# ELLWOOD TABLES

### for

## *Real Estate Appraising*

### *and*

## *Financing*

**Third Edition**

**Part I—Explanatory Text**

**Compiled for the
American Institute of Real Estate Appraisers
by
L. W. Ellwood, M.A.I.**

AMERICAN INSTITUTE OF REAL ESTATE APPRAISERS
155 East Superior Street, Chicago, Illinois 60611

*"All values are anticipations of the future."*
JUSTICE OLIVER WENDELL HOLMES

# PREFACE TO THE THIRD EDITION

Sudden and substantial changes in interest rates, lending policies and the spectre of inflation created a problem of keeping the capitalization tables up-to-date.

The obvious solution was to publish them in a loose leaf binder so new pages could be inserted as needed. On the other hand, tables of this type require a good deal of supplementary text covering directions for use and, since this material applies to principles of investment analysis and valuation which do not change, a separate, permanently bound volume was decided upon.

For these reasons, this edition comprises two volumes: (I) "Ellwood Tables for Real Estate Appraising and Financing—Explanatory Text," and (II) "Ellwood Tables for Real Estate Appraising and Financing" in ring binder. The tables have been expanded to include higher interest rates.

The reader's special attention is directed to the new "Cy" table. It has been recalculated to include a factor for investment analysis where it is natural to expect plus or minus changes in the income stream corresponding with future changes in property value. Its use is discussed and demonstrated in the explanatory text.

*L.W.E.*

# CONTENTS

## *Prologue*

## EXPERIENCE and JUDGMENT

*I believe experience can teach lessons which may lead to sound judgment. I believe sound judgment is vital in selecting the critical factors for appraisal. But, I also believe the bright 17 year old high school student in elementary astronomy can do a better job estimating the distance to the moon than the old man of the mountains who has looked at the moon for 80 years. So, I find it difficult to accept the notion that dependable valuation of real estate is nothing more than experience and judgment.*

*I would not give a red cent for an appraisal by the "expert" who beats his breast and shouts; "I don't have to give reasons. I've had 40 years experience in this business. And, this property is worth so much because I say so".*

*After all, value is expressed as a number. And, no man lives who, through experience, has all numbers so filed in the convolutions of his brain that he can be relied upon to choose the right one without explicable analysis and calculation.*

*L.W.E.*

# I

## THE CAPITALIZATION PROCESS

Chapter Three of the American Institute of Real Estate Appraisers' basic text: "The Appraisal of Real Estate," defines and discusses the ten principles of real property value.

Two of these principles cover the motivation for purchase and the basis for price negotiation.

1. *The Principle of Anticipation:*

   People buy real estate because they anticipate that ownership will provide them with certain future benefits.

2. *The Principle of Substitution:*

   Price is generally determined by the buyer's notion concerning the price at which he believes he could acquire substitute investments which would provide him with comparable benefits.

The other eight principles pertain to conditions the prudent buyer considers in estimating the nature, quality and magnitude of future benefits of ownership.

*Value* is therefore specifically defined as *the present worth of all rights to future benefits arising from ownership.*

To find value in dollars, according to this definition, the phrase "present worth" dictates that future benefits be estimated in dollars and discounted to present worth at rates of investment yield which will attract purchase capital.

This is the capitalization process. And, since future benefits must be expressed in dollars, it follows that the process applies in particular to the valuation of properties that produce dollar benefits in the form of rent and the proceeds of resale.

Other approaches are more applicable to properties in which the benefits of ownership are amenities of an aesthetic or emotional nature.

The first requirement for success in teaching any subject is mutual agreement between the text and the student as to the precise meaning of words and phrases. For this reason, semantics is especially important in a text on capitalization because it involves the use of language which may be interpreted in numerous ways.

## SEMANTICS:

The following definitions are presented to avoid misunderstanding as to the specific meaning of various terminology.

### Cash Market Value:

As used here, "cash market value" contemplates a transaction in which the seller would receive all cash in exchange for a clear and merchantable title to his property. This does not mean, however, that the buyer would not pledge such title to a financial institution as security for borrowing a major part of the purchase capital. The objective of the seller is to obtain the maximum amount of cash for his property. The buyer's source of funds is of no concern to him. The fact that mortgage money is available to typical buyers not only makes the real estate market what it is but the available amount, rate and term have a significant influence on the amount of cash the seller may obtain for good title. Therefore, realistic application of the capitalization process requires provision for normal composition and sources of purchase capital.

### Equity:

The amount or value of a property or properties above the total of liens or charges. When property is held free and clear, the owner is said to have a 100% equity. If 75% of purchase price is financed by mortgage, the buyer is said to acquire a 25% equity. Capital invested in any equity position whether it represents 100% or any fraction of value is known as risk or venture capital because there are no guarantees with regard to yield or recapture.

### Dividend Rate or Income Yield:

This is the ratio of net, annual cash flow income collected by the owner to his cash investment in the property.

### Investment Yield:

This is the total yield produced by both income and resale expressed as an annual rate of yield. In other words, it is the rate of interest at which the total present value of both income and reversion is equal to the cost of investment.

2

**Depreciation and Book Depreciation:**

"Depreciation" means total, actual decline in the market value of a property (including both land and improvements) from time of purchase to time of resale.

"Book Depreciation" means arbitrary, periodic reserves or allowances as set up against historical costs of wearing assets for purposes of cost accounting and income tax calculations. Since it pertains to historic costs only and is not affected by the movement of market values, it normally bears little relation to what actually happens in the market with regard to a given parcel of real estate.

**Recapture of Purchase Capital:**

This phrase is not to be confused with or considered as synonymous with depreciation.

In actual experience, recapture of purchase capital is usually accomplished by mortgage amortization and by sale of the equity position. Recapture of the mortgage component occurs according to terms of a periodic installment contract without regard to fluctuations in market value.

**Appreciation:**

This means increase in market value.

**Simultaneous Occurrence of Depreciation, Recapture and Appreciation:**

The following type of experience, which is not unusual, illustrates why it is essential to treat these three factors as separate amounts in realistic application of the capitalization process.

Smith purchased an income property for $150,000 and sold it ten years later for $135,000. He paid $50,000 cash and borrowed $100,000 on an installment mortgage contract. Amortization amounted to $35,000 reducing the loan balance to $65,000 and leaving Smith $70,000 as his share of the $135,000 proceeds of sale. During the term of ownership, depreciation amounted to 10 per cent, recapture by mortgage amortization amounted to 23⅓ per cent and the value of Smith's equity investment of $50,000 appreciated 40 per cent to $70,000.

The average net cash flow income produced by the property was $11,450 per year. The mortgage interest rate was 5 per cent. The composite capitalization rate was:

$$\frac{d}{v} = \frac{11,450}{150,000} = .0763 \text{ or } 7.63\%$$

3

The income distribution was:

| | |
|---|---:|
| Mortgage interest, $100,000 at 5% | $ 5,000 |
| Mortgage amortization, $35,000 × .00644 × 12 | 2,705 |
| Smith's average dividend | 3,745 |
| Total Income | $11,450 |

On a $50,000 investment, Smith collected income at $3,745 per year for ten years and a reversion of $70,000 at the end of that time. His average "dividend rate" was:

$$\frac{3,745}{50,000} = .0749 \text{ or } 7.49\%$$

His "investment yield" was 10 per cent as proved by the use of 10 per cent, ten years income and reversion factors as follows:

| | |
|---|---:|
| Income; $3.745 × 6.144567* | $23,012 |
| Reversion deferred 10 years; $70,000 × .385543* | 26,988 |
| Value of equity investment at time of purchase | $50,000 |

*Multipliers from 10% Compound Interest Table at 10 years. Cols. 5 & 4.

Thus, an over-all capitalization rate of .0763 provided for mortgage requirements, capital recapture, depreciation in property value and a 10% yield to the buyer.

**Annuities:**

An annuity is commonly thought of as a series of equal annual payments. The word is used here in a broader sense. The time interval between payments must be equal throughout the series but does not have to be a year. It may be a month, a quarter year, a half year or any other period of time. A common type is the "ordinary annuity" or "annuity in arrears" as represented by the series of payments in a level installment amortized mortgage contract where each payment is received at the end of each period. The "annuity in advance" or "annuity due" as represented by the series of payments provided by a lease requiring payment of rent at the beginning of each period will also be encountered. There will be problems involving declining annuities, increasing annuities and fluctuating annuities. In short, each type of periodic income stream may be considered as an annuity of one kind or another. Equal time intervals between payments is the only required characteristic. They can all be stabilized by formula to an equivalent "ordinary annuity."

4

## Coefficients:

A coefficient is any quantity to be used as a multiplier of another quantity. Standard coefficients for general and repeated use in the solution of various types of financial and engineering problems are precomputed and presented in tables.

A primary table is the "Table of Mortgage Coefficients." The six factors in standard "Compound Interest Tables" may also be used as coefficients or multipliers.

## The Sinking Fund Factor:

The sinking fund factor in combination with effective interest or yield rate is the most useful of all compound interest functions. It is used to calculate investment yield in the analysis of a composite capitalization rate.

It is used to determine the effect of depreciation or appreciation on present value. The periodic installment per dollar of mortgage money is the sinking fund factor for the full amortization term plus the effective interest rate. One or more sinking fund factors are integral parts of all capitalization rates except those pertaining to perpetuities. Sinking fund factors comprise Column No. 3 of the compound interest tables and applicable ones are included with the other tables.

## Reciprocals:

When one is divided by any number, the quotient is called the reciprocal of the given number. Since $1/4 = .25$ the reciprocal of 4 is .25. When any quantity is multiplied by the reciprocal of a given number, the product of multiplication will equal the quotient found when the same quantity is divided by the given number; i.e.;

$$16 \times .25 = 4$$

And

$$16 \div 4 = 4$$

The reciprocals of any two numbers are related to each other in reverse of the order in which the same numbers are related to each other; i.e.,

$$8 \div 4 = 2$$

whereas

$$1/4 \div 1/8$$

or

$$.25 \div .125 = 2$$

5

## Complements:

The complement of any fraction is the difference between the fraction and the whole number 1. The complement of 75% is 25% because $1 - .75 = .25$. If 30% of a mortgage loan is amortized, the unamortized balance will be the original amount multiplied by 70% which is the complement of 30%. If we call the total value of a property "V" in which $50,000 is allocated to land, the fraction of total value allocated to the building will be the complement of $\dfrac{\$50,000}{V}$ or $1 - \dfrac{50,000}{V} =$ fraction of "V" allocated to building.

If "V" happens to be $400,000 in this case, we will have:

$$1 - \frac{50,000}{400,000} = 1 - .125 = .875 \text{ or } 87\tfrac{1}{2}\%.$$

In other words, 87½% of total value is allocated to the building.

## Income Projection Term:

The existence of market value presupposes a market in which properties are bought and sold. If the tenure of ownership were total useful life, there would be no sales of improved income properties; hence, no market and no standards of comparison.

All commonly accepted definitions of market value contemplate a sale, at time of appraisal, *to one buyer*. It follows then that the projection term for appraisal should not attempt to cover more than one typical or optimum term of ownership.

As with any other form of investment, the timing of resale of income real estate has a very significant influence upon the yield. The investment yield may be raised two or three percentage points above the dividend yield if appreciation attributable to mortgage amortization, or any other cause, is taken advantage of during the first half dozen years. On the other hand, if the same property with the same dividend yield is held forty or fifty years, it will require several hundred times as much appreciation to produce the same investment yield.

Optimum terms of ownership have tended to become shorter in recent years because of changes in the monetary side of the market and the ever increasing impact of income taxes on take-home income.

Public records pertaining to many thousands of conventional income properties indicate that on the average this type of real estate changes hands or recasts its financing within ten years of purchase.

Aside from the obvious fact that a more reliable short term projection can be made than one purporting to cover total useful life, there are numerous other advantages.

The short projection will produce the same total value as a longer one, regardless of the capitalization technique so long as we assume the same income stream, the same rate of value change and the same rate of interest. In other words, any value loss due to the shorter income stream will be offset by a gain in the present value of the reversion. Thus, a five-year projection will produce the same value as a fifty-year projection when all other assumptions implicit in each projection are equal.

The short term projection offers a better chance for accuracy not only because the estimate of periodic income can be based on current facts and well-remembered experience but also because total value will not be attributable to income alone. A substantial portion of it will be due to residual value at the end of the projection. The law of compensating errors favors short projections.

The normal net cash flow income stream produced by landlord-serviced properties is one which fluctuates irregularly up and down from year to year. It does not follow a straight line path in either direction. A reasonably reliable estimate of average, annual net cash flow for a term of ten years or less can be treated as a level annuity with no significant error in the result. This has been proved by numerous case history tests pertaining to actual year by year earning records of office buildings, apartment projects, shopping centers, etc.

The most supportable over-all capitalization rate is one derived from comparable sales. It is relatively easy to test or analyze any over-all rate and interpret it in terms of probable yield to the equity investor when the projection is limited to ten years. It is virtually impossible to make such analyses when the projection is presumed to cover the total useful life of any structure which represents an appropriate use for its site at time of appraisal.

Therefore, projections in numerous examples of the uses of the various tables are confined to ten years. Longer projections are generally used only in cases involving long-term leases to financially responsible tenants. Since the duration of a specific income stream is fixed by contract, in such cases, it is advisable to employ the stipulated facts in preference to assumptions.

**Composite Capitalization Rate and
Overall Capitalization Rate**

These are synonymous terms. They both mean the same thing.

## STANDARD SYMBOLS:

Symbols, usually in the form of letters of the alphabet, are used to represent specific amounts or quantities. This avoids endless, time-consuming repetition in defining the factors presented in the statement of problems and in writing the equations by which they are solved.

Remember that each symbol dictates the use of a given number, and to solve any problem, all you need to do is substitute the proper number for each symbol and perform the operations in arithmetic indicated by the formula.

Standard symbols in common use are identified as follows:

**Y**  is the equity yield rate.

**I**  is the *annual* mortgage interest rate.

**i**  is the *effective* mortgage interest rate. It is the quotient found by dividing the annual mortgage interest rate by the number of installments per year. If installments are payable monthly; $i = I \div 12$. If installments are payable quarterly; $i = I \div 4$; etc. Note: Y, I and i are interest rates and may be interchangeable in compound interest formulas.

**f**  is the annual mortgage requirement per dollar of mortgage money including both interest and the provision for recapture or amortization. It is 12 times the monthly installment per dollar; etc. With interest at 5¼% per annum, the monthly installment including interest and provision for full amortization in 20 years or 240 months is quoted at $6.74 per month for each $1,000 of loan. The monthly requirement per dollar is $6.74 \div 1,000 = .00674$, and "f" in this case is $12 \times .00674 = .08088$. Obviously, "f" varies with each change in the mortgage interest rate and each change in the amortization term.

**M**  is the ratio of mortgage money to appraised value or to assumed total purchase price. If we assume 75 per cent of purchase price will be borrowed as mortgage money: $M = .75$. And, of course, "M" can be any ratio from zero to 100 per cent.

**C**  is the mortgage coefficient used in calculating a composite capitalization rate. When employed with equity yield "Y" and mortgage ratio "M," it provides for all ingredients of the composite capitalization rate except depreciation or appreciation in over-all property value. Table "C" presents a large selection of pre-computed coefficients with auxiliary factors for depreciation or appreciation. Tables "Ca," "Cp" and "Cy" are used for problems outside the scope of Table "C."

**P**   is the fraction of mortgage money which will be recaptured, amortized or "Paid Off" during the income projection term.

**Sm**   is the amount to which one dollar will grow including interest compounded at the effective mortgage interest rate over the entire term required for full amortization of a mortgage.*

**Sp**   is the amount to which one dollar will grow including interest compounded at the effective mortgage interest rate during the term of the income projection.*

$1/S_{\overline{n}|}$   is the symbol for a sinking fund factor at a given rate of interest for a given length of time. In most problems this will be at rate "Y" for a stated income projection term.

*Note: Factors represented generally by symbol "$S^n$" comprise Column No. 1 of the compound interest tables. This factor is sometimes called "the future worth of one dollar including interest."

**r**   is the basic capitalization rate which includes all the ingredients except provision for depreciation or appreciation during the income projection term. Since the mortgage component of purchase capital enjoys a secured position involving much less risk and management burden than the equity position, it will normally command a much lower interest rate than the prospective equity yield rate "Y." The equation for the basic rate is: the equity yield "Y" less the product of mortgage ratio "M" multiplied by mortgage coefficient "C," i.e.*

$$r = Y - MC$$

*Note: "r" is also used to represent the ratio of progression in the formula for the sum of a geometric progression.

**J**   adjustment factor to provide for gradual increases or declines in income. Table Cy.

## *Symbols*

**dep**  is the total amount of depreciation in over-all market value of property during the income projection term. Depreciation *increases* the over-all capitalization rate.

**app**  is the total amount of appreciation in over-all market value of property during the income projection term. Appreciation *decreases* the over-all capitalization rate.

**R**  is the over-all capitalization rate including depreciation or appreciation.

**d**  is the projected average, net cash flow income per year before mortgage installments.

**ed**  is the equity dividend rate, i.e., the ratio of cash flow to equity investment after mortgage installments.

**V**  is the present market value or assumed purchase price, i.e.,

$$\frac{d}{R} = V \text{ and, by transposition } \frac{d}{V} = R$$

## COMMON FORMULAS:

Common formulas in which these symbols are used follow. The next two chapters contain explanations and derivations.

Unless otherwise stipulated, the sinking fund factor is at equity yield "Y" for the income projection term in years.

*For Estimating Market Value, "V":*

$$r = Y - MC$$
$$R = r + \text{dep } 1/S_{\overline{n}|}$$
$$R = r - \text{app } 1/S_{\overline{n}|}$$
$$V = \frac{d}{R}$$

*For Computing Mortgage Coefficient, "C":*

$$C = Y + P \, 1/S_{\overline{n}|} - f$$

*For Computing "P" the Fraction of Mortgage Amortized During the Income Projection Term:*

$$P = \left(\frac{f}{I} - 1\right)(Sp - 1)$$

"Sp" the amount to which one dollar will grow in any number of periods is in Column No. 1 of the compound interest tables. Caution should be exercised in selecting this factor on the basis of the frequency of mortgage installments. In other words, use the monthly table where installments are monthly, the quarterly table when installments are quarterly, etc.

*Example:*

Compute "P" for 10 years where the annual requirement "f" is 7.56% including interest at 5¼% per annum and where installments are payable; (a) monthly, (b) quarterly, (c) semi-annually.

*Solutions:*

$$\text{Constant Multiplier} = \frac{f}{I} - 1 = \frac{.0756}{.0525} - 1 = .44$$

11

Sp — 1 from 5¼% compound interest tables at 10 years; Col. No. 1.

(a) Monthly; .688524 and P = .44 × .688524 = .30295
(b) Quarterly; .684695 and P = .44 × .684695 = .30127
(c) Semi-Annually; .679049 and P = .44 × .679049 = .29879

Note:

Since monthly installments will accelerate equity value build-up without increasing the mortgage requirement, monthly installments are usually assumed in computing the composite capitalization rate. "Sp — 1" factors for from 1 to 40 years on a monthly basis are presented in Table "Cp."

*To Compute the Annual Requirement "f" for Any Desired Amount of "P":*

$$f = \left(1 + \frac{P}{Sp - 1}\right)I$$

*Example:*

A lease will expire in 9 years. A mortgage commitment for $200,000 is to be 50 per cent amortized by the end of the lease term with interest at 5½ per cent per annum by monthly installments. Compute the monthly installment.

*Solution:*

P = .50; Sp — 1 at 5½%, 9 years monthly = .6386 from Table Cp.

$$f = \left(1 + \frac{.50}{.6386}\right).055 = 1.782963 \times .055 = .098063$$

Annual Requirements: $200,000 × .098063 = $19,612.58

Monthly Installment: $19,612.58/12 = $1,634.38

*To Calculate Value Change:* (depreciation or appreciation in over-all property value) which must occur during any income projection term for realization of any selected equity yield, "Y."

The basic rate "r" will increase as the equity yield "Y" increases. When the composite rate "R" is greater than "r," a decline in property value must occur to compensate for the difference in the two rates.

Thus: $\text{dep.} = \dfrac{R - r}{1/S_{\overline{n}|}}$

When equity yield "Y" is high enough to make basic rate "r" greater than composite rate "R," an increase in property value must occur to compensate for the difference.

Thus: $\text{app} = \dfrac{r - R}{1/S_{\overline{n}|}}$

Note: The above two formulas provide a practical method for analyzing any composite capitalization rate derived from market experience and interpreting it in terms of yield prospects for any equity investment. They are used in making the graphic analysis which shows value changes which must occur at any time during a projection for any yield within a selected range. For instruction and demonstration, see: "Problems Involving Use of Table C; (4) Estimating Prospects for Equity Yield."

*For Calculating the Full Amortization Term when "f" and "I" are stated:*

$$Sm = \frac{f}{f - I}$$

"Sm" is the amount to which one dollar will grow with interest at the effective rate "i" or the future worth of one dollar with interest for the full amortization term. This is in Column No. 1 of the Compound Interest Tables.

*Example:*

The annual constant mortgage requirement is 8 per cent including interest at $5\frac{1}{2}\%$. How long will it take to fully amortize the mortgage if installments are paid monthly?

*Solution:*

Stated factors: $f = .08$, $I = .055$

$$Sm = \frac{.08}{.08 - .055} = \frac{.08}{.025} = 3.2$$

Refer to $5\frac{1}{2}\%$ Monthly Compound Interest Table. Reading down the first column, the nearest factor below 3.2 is 3.165659 at 21 years, and:

$$\frac{3.2}{3.165659} = 1.0108479$$

The nearest factor above this quotient is at three months. Answer: 21 years and 3 months.

*Formulas*

*To Stabilize the Declining Income Stream Implicit in the Straight Line Depreciation Technique to the Equivalent Ordinary Annuity:*

$$\frac{d\,(Y + Nk\,1/S_{\overline{n}|})}{Y + k} = \text{ordinary annuity}$$

In which:

$d =$ first year income

$N =$ Projection term in years

$k =$ Annual straight-line depreciation rate

*Example:*

First year income "d" is \$19,000. Yield rate "Y" is 7%. Projection term "N" is 10 years. Straight line depreciation rate "k" is 2½%. Sinking fund factor at 7% 10 years is .0724.

Straight Line Valuation: $\dfrac{19,000}{.07 + .025} = \$200,000$

Annual Recapture at 2½%:   $\$200,000 \times .025 = \$\ \ 5,000$

Annual Income Decline:   $\$\ \ 5,000 \times .07 = \$\ \ \ \ 350$

Income will be \$19,000 the first year and decline \$350 each year thereafter.

*Problem:*

What ordinary annuity has the same present value as the first ten years of this declining income stream?

*Solution:*

$$19,000 \left( \frac{.07 + 10 \times .025 \times .0724}{.07 + .025} \right) = \frac{19,000 \times .0881}{.095} = \$17.619$$

14

*Arithmetic Check:*

Total depreciation in ten years would be 25 per cent of $200,000 or $50,000. Reversion deferred 10 years would be $150,000. Present value of income and reversion discounted 10 years at 7% must equal straight-line valuation of $200,000.

| | | |
|---|---|---|
| Income, | $17,619 × 7.023582 | $123,748 |
| Reversion, | $150,000 × .508349 | 76,252 |
| Total | | $200,000 |

Note: Coefficients are from Columns 5 and 4 of 7% Annual Compound Interest Table.

## GEOMETRIC AND ARITHMETIC PROGRESSIONS:

The capitalization process and the analysis of investments for prospective yields involve two types of quantitative series. Since each one may include a large number of quantities, formulae by which the sum or total of the series can be calculated are good time savers.

### Geometric Progression:—

This is any series in which all preceding or all succeeding quantities are related to each other by a constant multiplier called the "ratio of progression." The series of quantities whose sum comprises the Inwood Annuity Coefficient represents this type. While this can normally be found in a precomputed table, there are other geometric progressions which are not tabulated. An example would be the present value of a series of income tax deductions where reserves for depreciation are accumulated by any declining balance method. Another would be the total book depreciation which will be accrued by the declining balance method at any point in time.

The formula for the sum of a geometric progression is:

$$\frac{ar^n - a}{r - 1} = sum$$

in which

a = The smallest quantity in the series
r = The ratio of progression
n = The number of quantities in the series

15

Although derivation and uses of this formula are discussed in the next chapter, a word of caution is appropriate here: Make sure any series in question is in fact a geometric progression before application of the formula. This can be done by dividing several adjoining quantities to see if the ratio is constant.

### Arithmetic Progression:—

This is any series of quantities in which there is a constant difference between quantities. Examples are: the income stream implicit in the straight line depreciation capitalization technique and income tax deductions where reserves for depreciation are accrued by sum of the years digits method.

The formula for the sum of any arithmetic progression is:

$$\frac{n}{2}(a + L) = sum$$

in which

    n = Number of quantities in the series
    a = Smallest quantity in the series
    L = Largest quantity in the series

The following series is an arithmetic progression:

$$2 + 5 + 8 + 11 + 14 + 17 = 57$$

The constant difference is 3

$$n = 6, \quad a = 2, \quad L = 17$$

$$\frac{6}{2}(2 + 17) = 3 \times 19 = 57$$

# II

# CONSTRUCTION AND USE OF COMPOUND INTEREST TABLES

To understand the income approach, the appraiser must understand the arithmetic of compound interest. The reason this branch of arithmetic has remained a mystery, shunned by many people, is not because it is complex or hard to understand. Rather, it is because manual application is a tedious, time-consuming, and mentally exhausting process.

The electric calculator has eliminated this obstacle. Its use in conjunction with tables of pre-computed functions makes it possible to combine pertinent facts with realistic assumptions and solve problems in minutes which would otherwise consume many hours.

The critical factors in the income approach by any technique are amount, time, and investment yield. Although it should be obvious that every valid technique will produce the same result so long as these factors are equal, this is not always clear to the novice. Specific assumptions as to amount, time, and yield are implicit in each technique. These assumptions change more or less surreptitiously when a switch is made from one technique to another. The appraiser cannot make an intelligent selection of technique unless he knows exactly what the assumptions are and how they affect his result. Moreover, he cannot do a professional job with integrity unless he *believes* the assumptions implicit in the technique he selects. Otherwise, the appraisal will not be the result of his own judgment applied to pertinent facts. Instead it will be the product of a formula which may not be plausible in the light of relevant facts.

Every capitalization technique is a process for discounting anticipated future profits to present market value at yields which will attract purchase capital. The arithmetic of the process is the arithmetic of discount at compound interest. The objective of this chapter is to clarify this branch of arithmetic. The student appraiser will find the income approach by any technique readily understandable if he will take the time needed to absorb this subject.

There are two general classes of problems pertaining to the investment of capital for profit in the form of interest at a periodic rate. The first class concerns the amount to which a single sum or a series of future periodic installments will grow with the accumulation of interest at a fixed rate per period. The second class pertains to the present worth of a single sum to be collected at a specific future date or a series of future periodic installments for a specific number of periods when discounted from date of collection to the present time at a fixed rate of interest per period.

In each class there are three problem types. Hence there are six basic formulas. Since direct application of the formulas to each problem would consume a great deal of time, the formulas are employed for the compilation of standard tables. Each table presents six precomputed functions of one dollar at selected rates of interest for various periods of time. In other words, a lump sum of one dollar, or a series of one dollar installments, is assumed for calculation of each tabulated function. When the desired function for one dollar is known, it can be applied to any number of dollars by multiplication or division.

Thus a comprehensive, compound interest table presents six standard functions of one dollar. And since many problems involve the use of two or more of them it is most convenient to have them arranged in six columns on the same page for each effective interest rate. The "effective" interest rate is the quotient of the annual or "nominal" rate when divided by the number of conversion periods or installments per year. The user is, therefore, cautioned to select the appropriate conversion frequency. Do not use a monthly table when dealing with annual collections or annual compounding. The compound interest tables which supplement this text present functions computed for monthly, quarterly, semi-annual and annual collections or conversions for all nominal interest rates from 3 per cent to 12 per cent. The more speculative rates; i.e. from 13 per cent to 30 per cent, are presented on the basis of annual collections or conversions only.

The columns on each page are numbered from 1 to 6 and the identity of the function in each column with its formula and standard symbol is as follows:

## The Six Functions of One Dollar

### FUTURE VALUES:

*Standard*
*Formula    Symbol*

1. The amount to which an investment or deposit of one dollar will grow in a given number of time periods, including the accumulation of interest at the effective rate per period. This factor is commonly known as the *Future Worth of One Dollar with Interest.*

$$(1 + i)^n = S^n$$

2. The total accumulation of principal and interest of a series of deposits or installments of 1 dollar per period for a given number of periods with interest at the effective rate per period. This factor is commonly known as the *Future Worth of One Dollar per Period with Interest.*

$$\frac{S^n - 1}{i} = s_{\overline{n}|}$$

3. The level periodic investment or deposit required to accumulate one dollar in a given number of periods including the accumulation of interest at the effective rate. This is commonly known as the *Sinking Fund Factor.*

$$\frac{i}{S^n - 1} = 1/s_{\overline{n}|}$$

### PRESENT VALUES:

4. The present value of one dollar to be collected at a given future time when discounted at the effective interest rate for the number of periods from now to the date of collection. This is called the *Reversion Factor.*

$$\frac{1}{S^n} = V^n$$

5. The present value of a series of future installments or payments of one dollar per period for a given number of periods when discounted at the effective interest rate. This factor is commonly known as the *Inwood Ordinary Annuity Coefficient.*

$$\frac{1 - V^n}{i} = a_{\overline{n}|}$$

6. The level periodic installment which will pay interest and provide full amortization or recapture of an investment of one dollar in a given number of periods with interest at a given rate per period. Its most common application is as the periodic mortgage installment per dollar, and is in fact the *Ordinary Annuity which has a Present Value of One Dollar.*

$$\frac{i}{1 - V^n} = 1/a_{\overline{n}|}$$

Although the functions in columns 2, 3, 5, and 6 are computed on the basis of level periodic income, specific inter-relationships provide methods by which declining and increasing income streams can be readily converted or stabilized to a level income of equal value.

Please notice that $S^n$ or its reciprocal $V^n$ is the key factor in each formula. The only other quantities are "1" which represents 1 dollar and "i" which represents the "effective" interest rate. Thus, calculation of the quantity $S^n$ is the only one involving more than elementary arithmetic. Let us start the explanation by presenting the equation for it as follows:

$$S^n = (BASE)^{EXPONENT}$$

In which:

$S^n$     Equals the value to which one dollar will grow in a given length of time including the accumulation of interest at a given rate. Col. No. 1 Compound Interest Table.

The Base is one dollar plus the interest on one dollar for one interest conversion period of time; i.e. $(1 + i)$.

An interest conversion period is the time interval for which each interest collection or each interest accumulation is to be calculated.

In the United States, the interest rate is usually quoted as an annual rate called the "Nominal Rate."

The rate used in the base, however, is called the "Effective Rate."

The "Effective Rate" is found by dividing the annual or Nominal Rate by the number of interest conversion periods per year.

### Rule For Determining The Base

The Base is always one dollar plus the interest on one dollar at the "effective rate" for one conversion period.

### Assume for example an annual or nominal rate of 6%

If interest is to be converted annually, the interest on one dollar for 1 year is 6 cents and the base is 1.06. The "effective rate" is 6%.

If interest is to be converted semi-annually, the interest on one dollar for ½ year is 3 cents and the base is 1.03. The "effective rate" is 3%.

If interest is to be converted quarterly, the interest on one dollar for ¼ year is 1½ cents and the base is 1.015. The "effective rate" is 1½%.

If interest is to be converted monthly, the interest on one dollar for 1/12th year is one half cent and the base is 1.005. The "effective rate" is ½ of one per cent.

## The Exponent

The "Exponent" is the total number of conversion periods for which interest is to be accumulated at the effective rate. It is the number of times the base must be multiplied by itself to produce the sum "$S^n$"

Assuming a total term of 20 years with 6% as the nominal rate, each base with its exponent and resulting sum would be as follows:

| Conversion | Base & Exponent | | Col. 1 at 20 Years $S^n$ |
|---|---|---|---|
| Annually | $1.06^{20}$ | = | 3.207135 |
| Semi-Annually | $1.03^{40}$ | = | 3.262038 |
| Quarterly | $1.015^{80}$ | = | 3.290663 |
| Monthly | $1.005^{240}$ | = | 3.310204 |

Please note that although the annual interest rate is the same in all of the above examples, the value to which one dollar will grow changes with each variation in the frequency of conversion. The difference is not great with regard to one dollar but would be quite substantial if the original investment were a million dollars.

The formula in which the base and its exponent are usually written is:

$$(1 + i)^n$$

In which "i" is the effective rate of interest written as a decimal fraction of one dollar and "n" is the exponent.

## The Rule Of Exponents:

In a problem such as our last example where:

$$(1 + i)^n = 1.005^{240}$$

21

It would take a long time to multiply 1.005 by itself 240 times. This can be cut down to 9 steps however, by employing the rule of exponents as follows:

### WHICH EQUALS

| | | | | | |
|---|---|---|---|---|---|
| $1.005$ | $\times\ 1.005$ | $= 1.005^2$ | $1.005$ | $\times\ 1.005$ | $= 1.010025$ |
| $1.005^2$ | $\times\ 1.005^2$ | $= 1.005^4$ | $1.010025$ | $\times\ 1.010025$ | $= 1.020151$ |
| $1.005^4$ | $\times\ 1.005^4$ | $= 1.005^8$ | $1.020151$ | $\times\ 1.020151$ | $= 1.040707$ |
| $1.005^2$ | $\times\ 1.005^8$ | $= 1.005^{10}$ | $1.010025$ | $\times\ 1.040707$ | $= 1.051140$ |
| $1.005^{10}$ | $\times\ 1.005^{10}$ | $= 1.005^{20}$ | $1.051140$ | $\times\ 1.051140$ | $= 1.104896$ |
| $1.005^{20}$ | $\times\ 1.005^{20}$ | $= 1.005^{40}$ | $1.104896$ | $\times\ 1.104896$ | $= 1.220795$ |
| $1.005^{40}$ | $\times\ 1.005^{40}$ | $= 1.005^{80}$ | $1.220795$ | $\times\ 1.220795$ | $= 1.490338$ |
| $1.005^{80}$ | $\times\ 1.005^{80}$ | $= 1.005^{160}$ | $1.490338$ | $\times\ 1.490338$ | $= 2.221110$ |
| $1.005^{80}$ | $\times\ 1.005^{160}$ | $= 1.005^{240}$ | $1.490338$ | $\times\ 2.221110$ | $= 3.310204$ |

It should be noted that the exponent of the multiplier is added to that of the multiplicand in each step to determine the exponent of their product. Thus, if we know that:

$$1.005^{80} = 1.490338 \text{ and } 1.005^{160} = 2.221110$$

We also know that $80 + 160 = 240$ and, therefore:

$$1.005^{240} = 1.490338 \times 2.221110 = 3.310204$$

In multiplication, when exponents of a common base are added, their total is the exponent of the product.

In division, when numerator and denominator are expressed as a common base with exponents, the exponent of the quotient is found by subtracting the exponent of the denominator from that of the numerator. This is an important rule to remember because its use is required quite frequently in the capitalization process. To clarify it more emphatically, let us use the number "2" as a common base.

$$2 \times 2 = 2^2 = 4$$
$$2 \times 2 \times 2 = 2^3 = 8$$
$$2 \times 2 \times 2 \times 2 \times 2 = 2^5 = 32$$
$$2^2 \times 2^3 = 2^5 \text{ and } 4 \times 8 = 32$$
$$2^5 \div 2^3 = 2^2 = 4 \text{ and } 32 \div 8 = 4$$

**Exercises:**

(a) How many months will it take for an investment to double in value if the nominal rate is 6% and conversion occurs monthly?

We know that $1.005^n = 2$

By reading down the "amount of 1" column (Col. 1) we find the nearest number below 2 is 1.931613 which appears at 11 years or 132 months. Next, we divide 2 by this number.

$$\frac{(1+i)^n}{(1+i)^{132}} = \frac{2}{1.931613} = 1.035404$$

The nearest number to this quotient appears in the same column at 7 months. Since $132 + 7 = 139$, we know it will take approximately 139 months for the investment to double in value.

In other words, we find that:

$$1.005^{132} \times 1.005^7 = 1.005^{139}$$

and

$$1.005^{139} = 1.931613 \times 1.035529 = 2.000 +$$

(b) Find the value to which one dollar will grow in 12½ years at 6% interest per annum converted quarterly.

(Col. 1)

At 12 years, we find 2.043478. At 2 quarters which is ½ year, we find 1.030225.

Since our base is 1.015 and 12½ years is 50 quarter years, we know:

$$1.015^{50} = 2.043478 \times 1.030225 = 2.105242$$

**The Present Value of Future Collections:**

In exercise (b) we found that 1 dollar will grow to 2.105242 in 12½ years at 6% per annum compounded quarterly. Obviously then $10,000 in the same span of time and at the same rate would grow to:

$$2.105242 \times \$10,000 = \$21,052.42$$

Now, suppose a contract calls for payment of $100,000 in a lump sum 12½ years from today. The owner of this contract sells it on the basis of 6% interest per annum compounded quarterly. How much does he receive for the contract?

23

It is plain that he will receive the amount which will grow to $100,000 in 12½ years at 6% per annum compounded quarterly. And, this will be $100,000 divided by the amount to which 1 dollar will grow in 12½ years at the same rate, i.e.

$$\frac{\$100,000}{2.105242} = \$47,500.48$$

In other words, $47,500.48 × 2.105242 = $100,000. So the present value of $100,000 deferred 12½ years and discounted at 6% per annum compounded quarterly is $47,500.48. Moreover, the present value of 1 dollar deferred 12½ years at the same rate is:

$$\frac{1}{2.105242} = .4750048$$

Thus, the quantity .4750048 is the present value of each dollar deferred 12½ years at 6% per annum compounded quarterly and the present value of any given number of dollars discounted for the same length of time at the same rate is the product of the given number of dollars multiplied by .4750048; i.e.

$$\$100,000 \times .4750048 = \$47,500.48$$

In any case, where one is divided by a given quantity, the quotient is called the *"Reciprocal"* of the given quantity.

In this exercise .4750048 is the reciprocal of 2.105242. The amount $100,000 is called a *"Reversion."*

When $100,000 was divided by the base 1.015, converted 50 times, the quotient was $47,500.48. The same result was obtained by employing the reciprocal of the base converted 50 times as a multiplier of $100,000.

The present value of each dollar of any future reversion can, therefore, be represented by the following formula:

$$V^n = \frac{1}{(\textbf{BASE})^{\textbf{EXPONENT}}}$$

In which:

$V^n$    symbolizes the present value of each dollar of any reversion deferred "n" conversion periods. Column No. 4 Compound Interest Table.

**Development of the Annuity Coefficient:**

Let us now assume an effective rate of 25% in which case the base will be 1.25.

The present value of one dollar reversion deferred 1 period is:

$$\frac{1}{1.25} = .80 \text{ or } 80 \text{ cents}$$

The present value of a one dollar reversion deferred 2 periods is:

$$\frac{1}{1.25 \times 1.25} = \frac{1}{1.5625} = .64 \text{ or } 64 \text{ cents}$$

The present value of a one dollar reversion deferred 3 periods is:

$$\frac{1}{1.25 \times 1.25 \times 1.25} = \frac{1}{1.953125} = .512 \text{ or } 51.2 \text{ cents}$$

The present value of a one dollar reversion deferred 4 periods is:

$$\frac{1}{1.25 \times 1.25 \times 1.25 \times 1.25} = \frac{1}{2.44140625} = .4096 \text{ or } 40.96 \text{ cents}$$

An income stream of one dollar per period for four periods would comprise a series of 4 reversions of one dollar each. And the present value of the entire series can be summed up by employing the above factors as follows:

| | |
|---|---|
| Present Value of 1st dollar | .80 |
| Present Value of 2nd dollar | .64 |
| Present Value of 3rd dollar | .512 |
| Present Value of 4th dollar | .4096 |
| Total Value of Series | 2.3616 |

Since each item in this summation is the reciprocal of the base converted according to its respective exponent, it is apparent that the present value of the series can be expressed in this form:

$$\frac{1}{1.25} + \frac{1}{1.25^2} + \frac{1}{1.25^3} + \frac{1}{1.25^4} = 2.3616$$

or

$$.80 + .64 + .512 + .4096 = 2.3616$$

The series of 4 quantities left of the equal sign is what is known as a "geometric progression." In every series of this type, the ratio of progression will be the base. In other words, if we start with the smallest quantity .4096 and read from right to left, each quantity will be 1.25 times its predecessor. Therefore:

$$.4096 \times 1.25 = .512; \ .512 \times 1.25 = .64 \text{ and } .64 \times 1.25 = .80$$

Obviously, this is a very simple series involving only 4 reversions. However, if we had a 20-year, monthly conversion series, we would have 240 reversions and although the same method for determining total present value could be employed, it would be a very long process.

A quick method is provided by the following formula which produces the sum of any geometric progression regardless of the number of quantities in the series.

$$\frac{ar^n - a}{r - 1} = T$$

In which:

*In the Example*

$a =$ Smallest quantity in the series;      $\dfrac{1}{1.25^4} = .4096$

$r =$ Ratio of progression, i.e., the base;      $1.25$

$n =$ Number of quantities in series;      $4$

$T =$ Total of the series

Substituting these quantities for the symbols;

$$\frac{\dfrac{1 \times 1.25^4}{1.25^4} - \dfrac{1}{1.25^4}}{1.25 - 1} = T$$

$$\frac{1 \times 1.25^4}{1.25^4} = 1 \qquad \text{and,} \ \frac{1}{1.25^4} = .4096 = V^n$$

$$1.25 - 1 = .25 = i$$

So it boils down to:

$$\frac{1 - .4096}{.25} = \frac{.5904}{.25} = 2.3616$$

Therefore, the formula for the present value of any ordinary annuity of one dollar per period for any number of periods (i.e., the Inwood coefficient) is:

$$\frac{1 - V^n}{i} = a_{\overline{n}|}$$

26

An easy way to remember it is that it is the complement of the reversion factor divided by the interest rate.

$a_{\overline{n|}}$ is merely a standard symbol for the present value of an ordinary annuity of one dollar per period for "n" periods, where "i" is the effective interest rate.

It is commonly known as the "Inwood Coefficient" for an ordinary annuity. Column No. 5 Compound Interest Tables.

Now let us assume an income stream of $10,000 per period for four periods. We wish to know its present value at an effective rate of 25%. Since the present value of one dollar per period is 2.3616, the present value of $10,000 per period is:

$$\$10,000 \times 2.3616 = \$23,616$$

And the distribution of each $10,000 collection can be tabulated in this way:

| Period | Balance at Beginning of Period | Interest at 25% A | Principal Recapture B | Balance after Payment |
|---|---|---|---|---|
| 1 | $23,616 | $ 5,904 | $ 4,096 | $19,520 |
| 2 | 19,520 | 4,880 | 5,120 | 14,400 |
| 3 | 14,400 | 3,600 | 6,400 | 8,000 |
| 4 | 8,000 | 2,000 | 8,000 | 0 |
| | Totals | $16,384 | $23,616 | |

The amount in column (A) is always 25% of the unrecaptured balance shown in the first column.

The amount in column (B) is always what is left from $10,000 after payment of interest.

## The Future Worth of $1 per Period with Interest:

Notice that each succeeding amount from top to bottom in column "B" increases at the rate of 25% over its predecessor, i e.

$$4096 \times 1.25 = 5120; \; 5120 \times 1.25 = 6400; \; 6400 \times 1.25 = 8000$$

Another way to compute the total recapture would be:

$$4096(1 + 1.25 + 1.25^2 + 1.25^3)$$

which equals:

$$4096(1 + 1.25 + 1.5625 + 1.953125)$$

which equals:

$$\$4096 \times 5.765625 = 23,616$$

The series inside the parentheses is another geometric progression

$$1 + 1.25 + 1.25^2 + 1.25^3$$

In which:

"a," the smallest quantity is, 1
"r," the ratio is our base; 1.25
"n," the number of quantities is; 4

Thus, by formula:

$$\frac{ar^n - a}{r - 1} = total$$

We have:

$$\frac{(1 \times 1.25^4) - 1}{1.25 - 1} \qquad \text{which equals} \qquad \frac{2.441040625 - 1}{1.25 - 1}$$

which equals:

$$\frac{1.44140625}{.25} = 5.765625$$

The quantity 5.765625 is the total amount of principal and interest which would be accumulated if we deposited one dollar at the end of each period for 4 periods in an account which earned interest at the effective rate of 25%.

Hence, the progressive growth of principal recapture, as shown in Column "B" of our tabulation is precisely the same as if we deposited $4,096 at the end of each period for 4 periods with interest accumulating at the 25% effective rate. So if we multiply $4,096 by the accumulation of one dollar per period, the product is the original investment:

$$\$4,096 \times 5.765625 = \$23,616$$

This is exactly the manner in which the mortgage part of purchase capital is recaptured whenever part of the purchase price is financed by borrowing on a level installment basis.

## The Sinking Fund Installment:

In our example, the first payment in reduction of principal is $4096. We call this the "Sinking Fund Installment" because the growth and accumulation of a sinking fund is the same as that of one dollar per period deposited in an interest bearing account.

The sinking fund installment in an amortizing mortgage loan is that portion of the first periodic payment which is applied to reduction of principal.

The sinking fund installment is found by subtracting the first interest payment from the total periodic payment; i.e.

$$\$10,000 - \$5,904 = \$4,096$$

The formula which produced 5.765625 in our example was

$$\frac{(1 \times 1.25^4) - 1}{1.25 - 1} \quad \text{which equals} \quad \frac{1.25^4 - 1}{.25}$$

The same formula expressed in symbols is:

$$\frac{(1 + i)^n - 1}{i} = s_{\overline{n}|}$$

In which:

$s_{\overline{n}|}$ is a standard symbol for the accumulation of one dollar per period for any given number of periods including interest. $(1 + i)$ is the base and, of course, "n" is the number of installments in the series. (Column No. 2 Compound Interest Tables.)

If we know the amount of the sinking fund installment we can calculate the total amount of capital which will be recaptured at any time by multiplying the sinking fund installment by the accumulation of one dollar per period at the effective rate for the number of periods stated in the problem.

*Example:*

$200,000 of purchase price is financed by mortgage with interest at 5% per annum. Level quarterly installments of interest and principal are based on 7% per annum.

How much purchase capital will be recaptured by mortgage amortization at the end of 8 years?

*Solution:*

Annual 7% less 5% interest $= 2\%$. Quarterly sinking fund installment is:

$$\frac{\$200{,}000 \times .02}{4} = \frac{4000}{4} = \$1000$$

Find $s_{\overline{n}|}$ for 8 years in column 2 of 5% quarterly table.

*Answer:*

$1000 \times 39.050441 = \$39{,}050.44$.

### $1/s_{\overline{n}|}$ The Sinking Fund Factor:

This function of 1 dollar is the periodic sinking fund installment required to accumulate 1 dollar in a given number of periods including the accumulation of interest at a given rate per period.

It was previously demonstrated that 4 periodic installments of 1 dollar each with interest accumulated at an effective rate of 25% would grow to 5.765625. It follows then, that the periodic installment or deposit required to accumulate 1 dollar including interest at 25% in 4 periods is 1 dollar divided by 5.765625, i.e.

$$\frac{1}{5.76525} = .173442$$

If a sinking fund installment of .173442 is required to recapture an investment of 1 dollar, the sinking fund installment required to recapture $23,616 is $23,616 times .173442, i.e.

$$\$23{,}616 \times .173442 = \$4096$$

Thus, the sinking fund factor is the reciprocal of the future worth of 1 dollar per period with interest and is represented as such by the symbol: $1/s_{\overline{n}|}$

The formula as developed for $s_{\overline{n}|}$ is:

$$\frac{(1+i)^n - 1}{i} \text{ or } \frac{s^n - 1}{i} = s_{\overline{n}|}$$

The formula for its reciprocal is the inversion of that formula; i.e.

$$\frac{i}{(1+i)^n - 1} \text{ or } \frac{i}{s^n - 1} = 1/s_{\overline{n}|}$$

30

This factor comprises Column No. 3 of the compound interest tables. It has several very important uses. For one; the level periodic installment required to pay interest on and recapture each dollar of any investment is the sum of the effective interest rate and the sinking fund factor. With interest at 25% and the 4 year sinking fund factor at .173442, the combination is:

$$.25 + .173442 = .423442$$

It was found that the present value of $10,000 per period for 4 periods at 25% was $23,616. Conversely, the periodic installment required to pay interest on and recapture $23,616 in 4 periods would be:

$$\$23,616 \times .423442 = \$10,000$$

In most cases sinking fund recapture occurs at a lower rate of interest than the investment yield rate. This happens when purchase capital is composed of mortgage and equity money where the mortgage installments provide for recapture at a lower rate of interest than the prospective yield to equity. It may also happen in certain types of contracts where a recapture fund called the "depreciation reserve account" or "replacement reserve account" is required to be accumulated and held as a cash reserve. In this case, a level periodic sinking fund installment might be deposited in trust with a savings institution which would agree to credit and accumulate interest on it at a fixed contract or "safe rate." The technique involving recapture by this process is the same as used, for example, in the Hoskold Sinking Fund Method. It is appropriate to demonstrate the mechanics of it in discussing applications of the sinking fund factor.

Assume an investment of $100,000. The yield is to be 25 per cent and recapture is to be accomplished by depositing four level sinking fund installments in an account which will accumulate at 10 per cent interest. We have found that: $1.10^4 = 1.4641$

Thus:

$$s_{\overline{n}|} = \frac{(1+i)^n - 1}{i} = \frac{1.4641 - 1}{.10} = \frac{.4641}{.10} = 4.641$$

and $1/S_{\overline{n}|} = 1/4.641 = .215471$

Interest plus sinking fund per dollars is:

$$.25 + .215471 = .465471$$

Required periodic income is:

$$\$100,000 \times .465471 = \$46,547.10$$

31

Income distribution is:

Income per period.............................................. $46,547.10
Less Investment Yield; $100,000 × .25............... 25,000.00
Sinking Fund Installment............................. $21,547.10

Accumulation of Sinking Fund at 10%

$$\$21,547.10 \times 4.641 = \$100,000$$

The sinking fund factor will also be used later to reflect influence of future property value declines and increases on over-all capitalization rates and for interpreting comparative values in terms of probable yield to the buyer.

## $1/a_{\overline{n}|}$ The Ordinary Annuity Which Has a Present Value of 1 Dollar:

If 1 dollar per period for 4 periods at 25% has a present value of 2.3616, it is apparent that the level annuity which has a present value of 1 dollar is 1 dollar divided by 2.3616; i.e.

$$\frac{1}{2.3616} = .423442$$

Thus, we find that the total periodic installment required for interest and recapture is not only the sum of the interest rate and the sinking fund factor at that rate but it is also the reciprocal of the Inwood Ordinary Annuity Coefficient. The formula for this coefficient is:

$$\frac{1 - V^n}{i} = a_{\overline{n}|}$$

The formula for its reciprocal is the inversion of that formula:

$$\frac{i}{1 - V^n} = 1/a_{\overline{n}|}$$

This function is presented in column No. 6 of the compound interest tables. A common application of it is to calculate the periodic installment which will provide for interest and recapture in a level installment mortgage loan.

32

## Important Relationships of Compound Interest Functions:

Since the 1st column function "S"" is a key quantity in all formulas for the other 5 functions, it follows that the functions are all specifically related to each other. It is important to learn and remember a few of these relationships.

It has just been demonstrated that:

$$1/a_{\overline{n}|} \text{ is equal to } i + 1/s_{\overline{n}|}$$

$$.423442 = .25 + .173442$$

It is therefore apparent that:

$$1/a_{\overline{n}|} - 1/s_{\overline{n}|} = i; \quad .423442 - .173442 = .25$$

We found that, $1.25^4 = 2.44140625$

Other relationships are:

$$a_{\overline{n}|}(1+i)^n = s_{\overline{n}|}; \quad 2.3616 \times 2.44140625 = 5.765625$$

$$1/s_{\overline{n}|}(1+i)^n = 1/a_{\overline{n}|}; \quad .173442 \times 2.44140625 = .423442$$

Therefore:

$$\frac{1/a_{\overline{n}|}}{1/s_{\overline{n}|}} = (1+i)^n, \frac{.423442}{.173442} = 2.44140 \text{ etc.}$$

And, since $1/a_{\overline{n}|} - i = 1/s_{\overline{n}|}$

$$\frac{1/a_{\overline{n}|}}{1/a_{\overline{n}|} - i} = (1+i)^n$$

## To Review and Remember:

1. $1/a_{\overline{n}|} - 1/s_{\overline{n}|} = i$

2. $a_{\overline{n}|}(1+i)^n = s_{\overline{n}|}$

3. $\dfrac{1/a_{\overline{n}|}}{1/a_{\overline{n}|} - i} = (1+i)^n$

### To Compute Fraction of Purchase Capital Recaptured by Mortgage Amortization:

When the sinking fund installment per dollar is multiplied by the future worth of 1 per period with interest for any given number of periods (i.e. $s_{\overline{n}|}$) the product is the fraction of investment recaptured by amortization in the given number of periods.

Assume, for example, a mortgage component of purchase capital is to be fully amortized by "n" monthly installments of interest and amortization. A key lease expires in 8 years or 96 months and the fraction of mortgage to be amortized (call it "P" for "paid off") at lease termination is to be calculated.

The calculation expressed in basic formulas would be:

$$\left(\frac{i}{(1+i)^n - 1}\right)\left(\frac{(1+i)^{96} - 1}{i}\right) = P$$

Since numerator "i" in the multiplicand is the same as denominator "i" in the multiplier, they cancel out and the equation can be condensed to:

$$\frac{(1+i)^{96} - 1}{(1+i)^n - 1} = P$$

If the reciprocal of the denominator is used as a multiplier, the equation can be written as:

$$\left(\frac{1}{(1+i)^n - 1}\right) \times [(1+i)^{96} - 1] = P$$

Now assume monthly installments are based on a constant annual requirement of 9% including interest at 6% per annum.

Thus;

$$1/a_{\overline{n}|} = \frac{.09}{12} \text{ and } i = \frac{.06}{12}$$

By relationship you have memorized:

$$\frac{1/a_{\overline{n}|}}{1/a_{\overline{n}|} - i} = (1+i)^n$$

Thus;

$$\frac{\dfrac{.09}{12}}{\dfrac{.09}{12} - \dfrac{.06}{12}} = (1+i)^n = \frac{.0075}{.0075 - .005} = \frac{.0075}{.0025} = 3$$

Since the number of installments per year, "12" is a common denominator, it can be omitted without affecting the result; i.e.

34

$$(1 + i)^n = \frac{.09}{.09 - .06} = \frac{.09}{.03} = 3$$

Call the annual mortgage requirement per dollar "f" and the nominal interest rate "I." The amount to which 1 dollar will grow with interest at effective rate "i" during the full amortization term; i.e. $(1 + i)^n$ is always:

$$\frac{f}{f - I} = (1 + i)^n$$

In the above example:

$$(1 + i)^n = 3 \text{ and } (1 + i)^n - 1 = 2$$

The reciprocal of $(1 + i)^n - 1$, in this case is:

$$\frac{1}{2} = .50$$

This reciprocal in any case where "f" and "I" are known is:

$$\frac{f}{I} - 1 \text{ Thus; } \frac{.09}{.06} - 1 = 1.50 - 1 = .50$$

Call the amount to which 1 dollar will grow with interest in any income projection term "Sp." And, we have the formula:

$$\left(\frac{f}{I} - 1\right)(Sp - 1) = P$$

In the 6% *monthly* compound interest table (Column No. 1) $(1 + i)^n$ at 8 years or $(1 + i)^{96}$ is 1.614143.

Therefore; $Sp - 1$ is .614143 and;

$$P = \left(\frac{f}{I} - 1\right)(Sp - 1) = .50 \times .614143 = .307071$$

Suppose Mortgage is $160,000, the amount recaptured in 8 years will be:

$$P = \$160,000 \times .307071 = \$49,131$$

Arithmetic Check:

Level monthly installment; $160,000 × .0075.......... $1200.00
Interest, 1st month,

$160,000 × .005............ 800.00

Sinking fund installment................................. $ 400.00

$s_{\overline{n}|}$ at 8 years, Col. 2 in 6% *Monthly* compound interest table is 122.828542. Thus;

$$P = \$400 \times 122.828542 = \$49,131$$

35

When purchase capital is composed of equity and mortgage money, the fraction of mortgage recaptured (P) during an income projection term is a key factor in the composite capitalization rate. It is therefore, important to remember this formula for "P"

$$\left(\frac{f}{I} - 1\right)(Sp - 1) = P$$

## The Annuity In Advance:

Most real estate leases provide for payment of each installment of rent at the *beginning* of each period. The income stream provided by this type of contract is commonly known as the "annuity in advance" or "annuity due."

The "ordinary annuity" or "annuity in arrears" is represented by the series of payments provided by the level installment amortized mortgage contract where each installment is paid at the *end* of each period.

To convert the ordinary annuity coefficient to the "annuity in advance" coefficient, we must move each installment forward one period so each payment will be one period closer to the point of beginning. In other words, each installment will be subject to discount for one less period than each installment in the ordinary annuity. This conversion is accomplished by multiplying the ordinary annuity coefficient by its base.

The progression for an ordinary annuity of one dollar per period for 4 periods with interest at an effective rate of 25% is:

$$\frac{1}{1.25} + \frac{1}{1.25^2} + \frac{1}{1.25^3} + \frac{1}{1.25^4}$$

If we multiply this through by the base 1.25 we have:

$$\frac{1.25}{1.25} + \frac{1.25}{1.25^2} + \frac{1.25}{1.25^3} + \frac{1.25}{1.25^4}$$

And, by the rule of exponents, this equals:

$$1 + \frac{1}{1.25} + \frac{1}{1.25^2} + \frac{1}{1.25^3}$$

Or:

$$1 + .80 + .64 + .512 = 2.952$$

We found that the coefficient for the ordinary annuity for 4 periods at 25% effective rate is 2.3616. If we multiply it by the base;

$$1.25 \times 2.3616 = 2.952$$

The present value of $10,000 per period for 4 periods at an effective rate of 25% with each installment paid at the beginning of each period would be:

$$\$10,000 \times 2.952 = \$29,520$$

The distribution of each $10,000 collection can be tabulated as follows:

| Period | Balance at Beginning Of Period | Interest at 25% A | Principal Recapture B | Balance After Payment |
|--------|--------|--------|--------|--------|
| 1 | $29,520 | 0 | $10,000 | $19,520 |
| 2 | 19,520 | $ 4,880 | 5,120 | 14,400 |
| 3 | 14,400 | 3,600 | 6,400 | 8,000 |
| 4 | 8,000 | 2,000 | 8,000 | 0 |
| | | $10,480 | $29,520 | |

Notice that the entire amount of the first installment is applied to principal recapture. The reason for this is that since this payment is received at the beginning of the series, no time has elapsed for the accrual of interest. In effect, the buyer of the income stream is only out of pocket $19,520 at the point of beginning because he gets $10,000 back at the same time he pays $29,520 for the right to collect the series.

*Exercise:*

What is the present value of income from a 25 year net lease at $40,000 per year payable $10,000 quarterly in advance at a nominal rate of 6%.

*Solution:*

Quarterly Table at 6%, Col. 5. The ordinary coefficient at 25 years is 51.624704. The base is 1.015.

$$\$10,000 \times 1.015 \times 51.624704 = \$523,991$$

**The Declining Annuity:**

When provision for recapture of investment capital is made on the basis of straight line depreciation, it is automatically assumed that the income stream will also decline in a straight line. Although constant periodic

37

declines in values and income are not compatible with experience, provision for them is a safety factor which may protect against contingencies that do occur from time to time in market behavior and operating performance.

To facilitate the analysis of income real estate from the viewpoint of an equity investor, however, it is usually desirable to stabilize the income to an ordinary annuity of equal value.

To illustrate the principle of declining annuity valuation, let us visualize a 4 year income stream starting at $10,000 and declining at the rate of $562.50 per year. It can be diagrammed as set forth below:

|  | *Year 1* | *Year 2* | *Year 3* | *Year 4* |
|---|---|---|---|---|
| $ | 562.50 | | | |
| | 562.50 | 562.50 | | |
| | 562.50 | 562.50 | 562.50 | |
| | 562.50 | 562.50 | 562.50 | 562.50 |
| | 7750.00 | 7750.00 | 7750.00 | 7750.00 |
| Total | $10,000.00 | $9437.50 | $8875.00 | $8312.50 |

Reading the lines horizontally, the entire income stream is equivalent to 1 ordinary annuity of $7750 for 4 years plus 4 ordinary annuities of $562.50 from 1 to 4 years. Thus, $7750 multiplied by the Inwood co-efficient for 4 years plus $562.50 multiplied by the total of all Inwood coefficients from 1 to 4 will produce the present value of the series. The addition of 4 coefficients is simple enough but if the declining annuity ran 40 or 50 years, it would involve the addition of a long column of co-efficients. Therefore, a short-cut is desirable. Let us use 25% as the interest rate and write the series of 4 coefficients by formula:

$$\frac{1 - \dfrac{1}{1.25^1}}{.25} + \frac{1 - \dfrac{1}{1.25^2}}{.25} + \frac{1 - \dfrac{1}{1.25^3}}{.25} + \frac{1 - \dfrac{1}{1.25^4}}{.25}$$

Since the interest rate .25 is a common denominator, the series is equal to:

$$\frac{1 - \dfrac{1}{1.25} + 1 - \dfrac{1}{1.25^2} + 1 - \dfrac{1}{1.25^3} + 1 - \dfrac{1}{1.25^4}}{.25}$$

The numerator now comprises 4 positive quantities of 1 or a total of 4

38

(which is the number of annuities) less the progression for the Inwood coefficient. In other words, we have:

$$\frac{4 - \left(\dfrac{1}{1.25} + \dfrac{1}{1.25^2} + \dfrac{1}{1.25^3} + \dfrac{1}{1.25^4}\right)}{.25} = \frac{4 - 2.3616}{.25}$$

which equals; $\dfrac{1.6384}{.25} = 6.5536$

The total value of the declining annuity is therefore:

$$(\$7750 \times 2.3616) + (\$562.50 \times 6.5536)$$
$$= \$18,302.40 + \$3686.40$$
$$= \$21,988.80$$

Arithmetic Check:

| Year | Income | $V^n$ | Present Value |
|------|--------|-------|---------------|
| 1 | 10,000.00 × .80 | | $ 8,000.00 |
| 2 | 9,437.50 × .64 | | 6,040.00 |
| 3 | 8,875.00 × .512 | | 4,544.00 |
| 4 | 8,312.50 × .4096 | | 3,404.80 |
| Total Present Value: | | | $21,988.80 |

Therefore, where:

d = 1st period income

k = decline per period

N = number of periods

The present value of the declining annuity is:

$$(d - kN)\, a_{\overline{n|}} + \frac{k\,(N - a_{\overline{n|}})}{i} = V$$

The equivalent ordinary annuity is:

$$\frac{V}{a_{\overline{n|}}}$$

When the formula for V is divided through by the Inwood coefficient it boils down to:

$$d - \frac{k(1 - N\,1/s_{\overline{n}|})}{i} = \frac{V}{a_{\overline{n}|}}; \text{ i.e. } \frac{\$21,988.80}{2.3616} = \$9310.98$$

In which, $1/s_{\overline{n}|}$ is the sinking fund factor at rate i for N periods. In this case the sinking fund factor is .173442

$$\$10,000 - \$562.50\,\frac{(1 - 4 \times .173442)}{.25} =$$

$$\$10,000 - \$689.02 = \$9310.98$$

$$\$9310.98 \times 2.3616 = \$21,988.80$$

When straight line depreciation is quoted at a percentage rate per year, call the depreciation rate "k" and compute the amount to be subtracted from 1st year income "d" as follows:

$$\frac{dk(1 - N\,1/s_{\overline{n}|})}{i}$$

Say 1st year net income "d" is $50,000, the depreciation rate "k" is 2½%, the interest "i" is 10% and the income projection term "N" is 10 years. $1/s_{\overline{n}|}$ for 10 years at 10% (Col. 3 Compound Interest Table) is .062745. The multiplier of $50,000 is:

$$.025\,\frac{(1 - 10 \times .062745)}{.10} = .025\frac{(.37255)}{.10} = .0931375$$

| | |
|---|---|
| 1st year income | $50,000.00 |
| Less adjustment for decline; $50,000 × .0931375 | 4,656.88 |
| Level annuity of equal value | 45,343.12 |

If gross rent with present occupancy is $93,000, a vacancy allowance of 5% would provide a safety factor equal to that implicit in the 2½% depreciation rate, i.e., $93,000 × .05 = $4650.

## The Increasing Annuity:

A 4 period annuity starting at $100 and increasing $100 per period can be diagrammed for valuation as follows. The underscored installments $100 are added to produce a constant annuity for the 1st step. Their present value is then subtracted leaving the present value of actual installments to be received.

40

| Period | 1 | 2 | 3 | 4 |
|--------|-----|-----|-----|-----|
| | 100 | 100 | 100 | 100 |
| | 100 | 100 | 100 | 100 |
| | 100 | 100 | 100 | 100 |
| | 100 | 100 | 100 | 100 |
| | 100 | 100 | 100 | 100 |

Using reversion factors with interest at 25% we would have:

Present Value 1st installment 100 × .80...................... $ 80.00

Present Value 2nd installment 200 × .64 ................. 128.00

Present Value 3rd installment 300 × .512.................. 152.60

Present Value 4th installment 400 × .4096................ 163.84

Total Present Value of the Series ............. .............. $525.44

*Formula:*

Call periodic increase "h"; Number of Installments "N"; First Installment "d."

$$(d + hN)a_{\overline{n}|} - h\frac{(N - a_{\overline{n}|})}{i} = \text{Present Value}$$

By formula for present value of the 4 period straight line increasing annuity:

100 + (4 × 100) = 500

500 × 2.3616 ............... ................................... $1,180.80

Less 100 $\frac{(4 - 2.3616)}{.25}$ = 100 × 6.5536 .............. 655.36

$ 525.44

*Exercise:*

What is the present value at 6% effective of a 40 period straight line increasing annuity which starts at $4,000 the first period and increases $100 each period thereafter?

*Solution:*

If we multiply $100 by 40 and add the $4,000 product to our $4,000 initial period installment the total is $8,000. And, the present value of the entire income stream will be the present value of $8,000 per period for 40 periods less the present value of 40 annuities of $100 each for terms of 1 to 40 periods. (Factor from column 5 at 40 periods 15.046297.)

$8,000 \times 15.046297$ ............................................... $120,370

Less $100 $\dfrac{(40 - 15.046297)}{.06}$ $= 100 \times 415.89505$    41,590

Present Value of the Increasing Annuity................... $\overline{\$\ 78{,}780}$

## Other Variable Annuities:

Many complicated problems can be divided into two or more simple problems. This is especially true in the valuation of future income streams which are expected to increase or decline.

Step up and step down leases are not uncommon.

Valuation of such income streams can usually be simplified by dividing them into ordinary annuities.

(A) What is the present value at 6% of the income provided by a net lease as follows assuming rent is payable monthly in advance?
    1st 3 years.............................................................. $6,000 per year
    Next 5 years........................................................... $7,200 per year
    Last 12 years .......................................................... $8,100 per year

*Solution:*

The total term is 240 months:
The highest rent is $675.00 per month.
The middle term rent is $600.00 per month.
The first term rent is $500.00 per month.
The entire stream is equal to a 240 monthly annuity at $675.00 *less* 2 annuities for 36 and 96 months at $100.00 and $75.00 respectively.

Problems of this type can usually be visualized most clearly by diagram. A suggested method is to surround areas representing annuities to be received by solid lines and those to be subtracted by dotted lines.

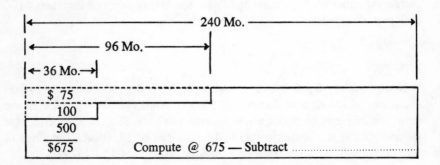

| | | | | | |
|---|---|---|---|---|---|
| | 240 months | $675 × 139.580771 | | | $94,217.02 |
| Less | 36 months | 100 × 32.871016 | $3,287.10 | | |
| and | 96 months | 75 × 76.095218 | 5,707.14 | | 8,994.24 |
| | Value as ordinary annuities | | | | $85,222.78 |
| | Times Base | | | | 1.005 |
| | Value as Annuities in advance | | | | $85,648.89 |

(B) A property is leased at $48,000 net per year payable $4,000 monthly in advance for 25 years with 2 renewal options. The 1st option is for 15 years with rental at $3,500 monthly in advance. The 2nd option is for 10 years with rental at $3,000 monthly in advance.

What is the value of this income at 6% if both options are exercised by the tenant?

*Solution:*

This is the equivalent of 1 annuity of $3,000 per month for 600 months, plus 2 annuities of $500 per month for 480 and 300 months.

| | | |
|---|---|---|
| 600 months; $3,000 × 189.967874 | | $569,903.62 |
| 480 months; 181.747584 | | |
| 300 months; 155.206864 | | |
| 336.954448 × 500 | | 168,477.22 |
| Value as ordinary annuity | | $738,380.84 |
| Times Base | | 1.005 |
| Value as annuity in advance | | $742,072.74 |

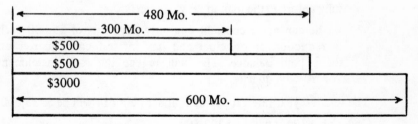

(C) What is the value at 6% of an annuity in advance of $6,000 per month for 10 years starting 5 years from today?

43

*Solution:*

This is equivalent to a monthly annuity in advance of $6,000 for 15 years or 180 months less one of the same amount for 60 months.

> 180 months; 118.503514
>
> Less  60 months;  51.725561
> _____
>
> 66.777953 × $6,000 .......... $400,667.72
>
> Times base ................................... 1.005
> _____
>
> Value as annuity in advance........................... $402,671.06

The effect of subtracting the 60 month factor from that for 180 months is that of deferring a 10 year factor 60 months. Another method would be to multiply the 10 year column 5 factor by the 5 year column 4 factor and the base.

$$90.073453 \times .741372 \times 1.005 \times \$6,000 = \$402,671$$

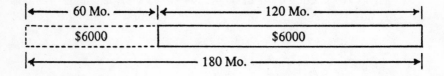

(D) A property is leased for 20 years at a net rental of $42,000 per year payable $3,500 monthly in advance. A buyer can borrow $400,000 of the purchase price at 5%. He has the choice of two 20 year amortization plans.

    (1) He can pay level monthly installments of $2,640 which will fully amortize the loan in 20 years.

    (2) Or he can make constant quarterly payments of $5,000 each in reduction of principal and pay interest each quarter on the unpaid balance. This will reduce the total installment $62.50 each quarter.

The total 20 year interest payment under plan (1) will be $233,600.

Under plan (2) it will be $202,500.

Which plan will produce the greatest value for the equity position on the basis of an 8% equity yield?

*Solution:*

Factors from column 5. 240 month annuity adjusted in payment in advance:

at 8% $3,500 × 1.00666666 + = 3523.33

| | |
|---|---|
| Plan (1) .............................................. | $3,523.33 |
| Less ordinary annuity ............................ | 2,640.00 |
| 119.554291 × ................................ | $ 883.33 |
| = Value of Equity Income.................................................. $105,606 | |

Plan (2)

In this case the mortgage installments will be a straight line declining annuity starting at $10,000 and declining $62.50 each quarter to the 80th quarter. This is equivalent to an 80 quarter ordinary annuity of $5,000 per quarter plus 80 ordinary annuities of $62.50 for from 1 to 80 quarters.

Present value of total income stream at 8%:

| | | |
|---|---|---|
| $3,523.33 × 119.554291 ................................ | | $421,229 |
| Less $5,000 × 39.744514 ...................... | $198,723 | |
| 62.50 × 2012.7743 ...................... | 125,798 | 324,521 |
| Value of Equity Income ...................................... | | $ 96,708 |

It is noteworthy that despite the larger mortgage interest obligation in Plan (1), this plan produces a greater equity value than Plan (2). The reason is that several years must pass before residual income to equity in Plan (2) catches up with the level equity annuity provided by Plan (1). And, since present dollars are worth so much more than future dollars, the aggregate interest advantage of Plan (2) is more than offset by the time advantage to equity in Plan (1).

The multiplier 2012.7743 by which we determine the present value of the series of $62.50 drops in quarterly mortgage installments is the total of all Inwood ordinary annuity coefficients from 1 period to 80 periods at the effective quarterly rate of 2%, i.e. 8% divided by 4.

The formula by which this multiplier is calculated is as follows:

$$\frac{80 - 39.744514}{.02} = \frac{40.255486}{.02} = 2012.7743$$

The factor 39.744514 is in column 5 at 80 quarters.

## USE OF THE RULE OF EXPONENTS FOR TABULAR EXPANSION:

The future worth of one dollar with interest "$S^n$" (Column No. 1) and its reciprocal "$V^n$" (Column No. 4) can be expanded by direct application of the rule of exponents. Use of this rule with the formula for each function facilitates tabular expansion. Each monthly compound interest table, for example, presents each function for each of the first eleven months. After that, they are presented by the year for 1 to 50 years. This provides on one page all quantities needed to find any function for any number of months from 1 to 600. Assume for instance, we wish the six functions at a nominal rate of 6 per cent converted monthly for nineteen years and seven months. Needed factors from Columns 1 and 4 of the 6% *monthly* compound interest table are:

Column No. 1 at 7 months 1.035529; at 19 years 3.117899

7 months $+$ 228 months $=$ 235 months

$(1.005)^{235} = 1.035529 \times 3.117899 = 3.228675$

Column No. 4 at 7 months, .965690; at 19 years, .320729

$$\frac{1}{(1.005)^{235}} = .965690 \times .320729 = .309725$$

Complement $= 1 - .309725 = .690275$

Future worth of 1 per period:

$$\frac{S^n - 1}{i} = \frac{2.228675}{.005} = 444.735$$

Sinking Fund Factor:

$$\frac{i}{S^n - 1} = \frac{1}{444.735} = .002243$$

Inwood Coefficients:

$$\frac{1 - V^n}{i} = \frac{.690275}{.005} = 138.055$$

Monthly Installment Factor:

$$\frac{i}{1 - V^n} = \frac{1}{138.055} = .007243.$$

or $i + 1/S_{\overline{n}|} = .005 + .002243 = .007243$

46

## For Expansion Beyond Scope of Table:

The same rule applies for expansion to a greater number of periods than shown by the table. For example, a ninety-nine year ground lease provides net rent at $54,000 per year payable $13,500 quarterly in advance. What is the present value of this income stream at 6% per annum? Factors from 6% *quarterly* compound interest table Column No. 4 at 39 years, .098016; at 60 years, .028064. 156 quarters + 240 quarters = 396 quarters.

$$\frac{1}{(1.015)^{396}} = .098016 \times .028064 = .0027507$$

Complement = 1 — .0027507 = .9972493
Inwood Ordinary Coefficient:

$$\frac{1 - V^n}{i} = \frac{.9972493}{.015} = 66.483287$$

Answer:

$$\$13,500 \times 1.015 \times 66.483287 = \$910,987.$$

It is noteworthy that the quarterly in advance feature makes present value of income before reversion greater than would be produced by the common practice of treating long term lease income as a perpetuity which assumes a 100 per cent reversion.

$$\frac{54000}{.06} \text{ or } \frac{13500}{.015} = \$900,000$$

## AMORTIZATION AND DEPRECIATION SCHEDULES

There are occasions when it is desirable to know the amount of capital which will be recaptured through mortgage amortization each year. A schedule of this type is sometimes compiled in conjunction with one showing annual depreciation allowances under various methods permitted by Internal Revenue Service. This is done to determine the extent to which amortization installments may be sheltered against income taxes by allowable deductions.

*Example:*

Appraised Value or Purchase Price:

| | |
|---|---:|
| Land | $ 100,000 |
| Building | 900,000 |
| Total | $1,000,000 |

Assumed Purchase Capital Structure:

| | |
|---|---:|
| 75% Mortgage (5%, 20 yrs. Monthly) | $ 750,000 |
| 25% Cash Equity | 250,000 |
| Total | $1,000,000 |

*Problem:*

Prepare an annual schedule showing amortization and depreciation based on 30 year building life, 150% declining balance basis. Carry schedule to the year in which amortization will exceed the allowance for depreciation.

*Solution:*

The monthly installment per dollar of mortgage with interest at 5% and full amortization in 20 years by level monthly installments is .0066 (Col. 6 at 20 years).

| | |
|---|---:|
| Monthly installment $750,000 $\times$ .0066 | $4,950 |

Less: 1st interest payment:

$$\frac{750,000 \times .05}{12} = \frac{37500}{12} \qquad 3,125$$

| | |
|---|---:|
| Sinking fund installment | $1,825 |

Amortization, 1st year (2nd column at 1 year times sinking fund installment).

$$12.278855 \times 1825 = \$22,408.91$$

The construction of the 1st year multiplier is:

$$1 + S + S^2 + S^3 + S^4 \text{ etc. to } S^{11}$$

The 2nd year multiplier will be the series of 12 quantities from $S^{12}$ to $S^{23}$ inclusive.

If we multiply the 2nd column factor at 1 year by the 1st column factor at 1 year we will have our 2nd year multiplier.

$S^{12} (1 + S + S^2 + S^3$ etc. to $S^{11})$ which will equal:

$$S^{12} + S^{13} + S^{14} \text{ etc. to } S^{23}$$

The 3rd year multiplier will be the series of 12 quantities from $S^{24}$ to

$S^{35}$. Thus, if we multiply our 2nd year multiplier by the 1st column factor at 1 year, we will have the 3rd year multiplier:

$$S^{12} (S^{12} + S^{13} + S^{14} \text{ etc. to } S^{23}) = S^{24} + S^{25} + S^{26} \text{ etc. to } S^{35}$$

Now, it is apparent that if we continue to use $S^{12}$ as a constant multiplier of the product for each preceding year, we can produce a schedule showing the amount of amortization each year. $S^{12}$ the 1st column factor at 1 year is 1.051162.

| | | |
|---|---|---|
| 1st year amortization as computed | | $22,408.91 |
| 2nd year | 1.051162 × $22,408.91 | 23,555.39 |
| 3rd year | 1.051162 × 23,555.39 | 24,760.53 |
| 4th year | 1.051162 × 24,760.53 | 26,027.33 |
| And, so on. | | |

The allocation to building is $900,000. The 30 year life straight line depreciation rate would be 3⅓%. The 150% declining balance rate would start at 1½ times 3⅓% or 5% and the amount of depreciation for each succeeding year would be 5% of the undepreciated balance. In other words, the depreciation allowance will decline at the rate of 5% per year. The 1st year depreciation allowance will be 5% of $900,000 which is $45,000 and we must use 0.95 as a constant multiplier to determine the allowance for each succeeding year. Therefore, the schedule would be as set forth below:

| Year | A Amortization | B Depreciation | B-A Surplus Shelter | |
|---|---|---|---|---|
| 1 | $ 22,408.91 | $ 45,000.00 | $22,591.09 | |
| 2 | 23,555.39 | 42,750.00 | 19,194.61 | |
| 3 | 24,760.53 | 40,612.50 | 15,851.97 | |
| 4 | 26,027.33 | 38,581.87 | 12,554.54 | |
| 5 | 27,358.93 | 36,652.78 | 9,293.85 | Total |
| 6 | 28,758.66 | 34,820.13 | 6,061.47 | surplus |
| 7 | 30,230.00 | 33,079.12 | 2,849.12 | $88,396.65 |
| 8 | 31,776.63 | 31,425.16 | Deficit 351.47 | |
| | $214,876.38 | $302,921.56 | $88,045.18 | |

The tabulation shows that not only will all amortization payments be sheltered against income taxes during the 1st 7 years but the owner would also realize over $88,000 of surplus shelter for other income during this period. If he retains ownership beyond 7 years, he will be liable for a rather rapidly increasing amount of tax on amortization installment unless he refinances. It is apparent that the optimum term of ownership in this case would be something less than 8 years.

### Computing the Amortization for a Specific Period

The sinking fund installment in the foregoing example is $1,825. Starting with 1 to represent the 1st or sinking fund installment, the series of succeeding installments will grow as follows:

| Installment No. | 1 | 2 | 3 | 4 | 5 etc. |
|---|---|---|---|---|---|
| Amount | 1 | S | $S^2$ | $S^3$ | $S^4$ etc. |

Since the exponent at each period is 1 less than the position of the installment in the series, we can calculate the amount of principal in any periodic installment by using the column 1 factor at 1 period less as a multiplier of the sinking fund installment. In other words, the sinking fund installment multiplied by $S^{68}$ would produce the amount of principal in the 69th periodic payment.

Since $S^{68}$ is the product of $S^8$ and $S^{60}$ Col. 1 the 69th amortization installment in our example would be as follows:

$$\$1,825 \times 1.033824 \times 1.283359 = \$2,421.35$$

Amortization which will occur in any year can be calculated by multiplying the 1st year amortization by the column 1 factor at 1 year less than the year for which amortization is to be determined. First year amortization in our example is $22,408.91. If we wish to know the amount of amortization to be paid during the 7th year, we multiply this by the column 1 factor at 6 years.

$$1.349018 \times \$22,408.91 = \$30,230$$

The reason for this is that the 1st year series of quantities is represented as follows:

$$1 + S + S^2 + S^3 \text{ etc. to } S^{11}$$

The 7th year will be the 12 quantities:

$$S^{72} + S^{73} + S^{74} \text{ etc. to } S^{83}$$

The 1st column factor at 6 years is $S^{72}$. Thus, by multiplying the 1st year we have:

$$S^{72} (1 + S + S^2 + S^3 \text{ etc. to } S^{11}) = S^{72} + S^{73} + S^{74} \text{ etc. to } S^{83}$$

50

# III

## INVESTMENT YIELDS AND CAPITALIZATION RATES

The combination of debenture and risk capital which supplies the monetary requirements of the real estate market presents two completely different problems with regard to the determination of investment yield.

The interest rate or yield and the provision for recapture are specifically stipulated by contract with regard to the mortgage or debenture money involved in market transactions.

A directly opposite set of conditions presents itself with regard to the equity or risk component of purchase capital. Both recapture and interest rate are entirely speculative at the time of investment. In fact, the interest or yield rate is never known until the complete investment experience is a matter of history. It cannot be calculated until *after* the property has been bought, operated over a span of time and then resold.

Consequently, it is incorrect to say that buyers demand this or that yield. The only plausible and supportable opinion is that "good prospects" for a yield of Y% or better would probably attract a buyer.

The yield on equity investment will be significantly influenced by the source of recapture, and this in turn will be determined by the relative magnitudes of periodic income and proceeds of resale or "reversion."

1. If reversion is less than original investment, part of the recapture must be taken from periodic income leaving only the remainder income as yield producing profit.

2. If the reversion is equal to the original investment, all of the recapture will be in the reversion and all of the periodic income will be yield producing profit.

3. If the reversion is greater than the original investment, all of the recapture will be in the reversion and the balance of the reversion plus all of the periodic income will be yield producing profit.

4. If the aggregate total of reversion and all periodic income is equal to or less than the original investment, there will be no profit and no yield.

51

Obviously, one of these sets of conditions will occur. Which one, when and to what extent is never known at time of purchase.

The equity position may represent 100% of value as in the all-cash-out-of-pocket market transaction. Or, it may be very thin with virtually all purchase capital in the form of mortgage money.

Obviously, the risk of equity investment increases as it gets thinner. A relatively small decline in the market will wipe out a 5% equity, whereas the 100% equity will survive so long as the property retains any value at all.

Since risk is a prime factor in determining the market attractiveness of any prospective yield, it follows that the prospective yield to equity must increase as the ratio of mortgage to value increases; which is to say that the availability of a large amount of mortgage money does not necessarily increase market value. If there is an increase in value, it will be more attributable to keen competition between mortgage investors driving interest rates down, plus the fact that plenty of cheap money will increase the number of prospective buyers.

Many buyers who are capable of paying all cash out of pocket are attracted to the fractional equity by leverage and by income tax shelter. A 10% increase in property value appreciates the value of a 25% equity by 40%.

When mortgage installments are paid from property income, the value of the equity position increases to any extent that mortgage amortization exceeds decline in over-all market value of the property. Thus, "appreciation" in equity value can occur simultaneously with "depreciation" in property value. And, since equity yield is properly defined as the interest rate at which the total present value of equity income and equity reversion is equal to the cost of the investment, it is clear that equity value build-up by reason of mortgage amortization may have a significant influence on equity yield.

Assume the following circumstances, for example:

A property is purchased for $400,000, of which $300,000 is financed by mortgage in which monthly installments are based on 8% per annum including interest at 5½%. The equity investment is $100,000. This property is resold 10 years after purchase for $340,000. The equity reversion can be calculated in this manner:

Sp — 1 at 10 years from Col. 1. 5½% *Monthly* Table = .731076

$$P = \left(\frac{.08}{.055} - 1\right).731076 = .454545 \times .731076 = .332307$$

| Selling Price (Property Reversion) | | $340,000 |
|---|---|---|
| Original Mortgage | $300,000 | |
| Less Amortization, $300,000 × .332307 | 99,692 | |
| Unamortized balance at time of sale | | $200,308 |
| Reversion to Equity | | $139,692 |

Despite 15% decline in property value, the value of equity increases almost 40%.

*Exercise:*

With purchase price and depreciation as above:
- (a) What stabilized annual cash flow income would provide for mortgage requirements and give the buyer a 10% yield on his $100,000 investment?
- (b) What composite capitalization rate is indicated by the answer to (a)?
- (c) Allocate the composite capitalization rate to the mortgage and equity components of purchase capital.

*Solution:*

| (a) Mortgage Requirement $300,000 at 8% | | $24,000 |
|---|---|---|
| Equity Investment | $100,000 | |
| Less Pres. Val. Reversion | | |
| $139,692 × .385543 | 53,857 | |
| Required Pres. Val. Equity Income | $ 46,143 | |
| Multiply by Instal. factor Col. 6 | .162745 | *7,510 |
| Total Annual Income Requirement | | $31,510 |

(b) Indicated Composite Capitalization Rate:

$$\frac{31,510}{400,000} = .078775$$

*Use of the installment factor as a multiplier produces the ordinary annuity which has a present value of $46,143.

(c) Allocation:

| Mortgage Money, 75% at .08 | .060000 |
|---|---|

Equity dividend rate, $\frac{7510}{100,000} = .0751$

| Equity money, 25% at .0751 | .018775 |
|---|---|
| Composite | .078775 |

## Symbol "Y"

Symbols "I" and "i" have been used to represent nominal and effective interest rates respectively up to this point in the text. A new symbol, "Y," is now introduced to represent equity yield and to distinguish the interest rate on risk capital from that on debenture capital. This makes no difference in rules pertaining to the relationship of compound interest functions.

$(1 + Y)^n$ is the base to the "n"th power.

$$a_{\overline{n}|} (1 + Y)^n = s_{\overline{n}|} \text{ at } Y$$
$$1/a_{\overline{n}|} - 1/s_{\overline{n}|} = Y$$

The composite capitalization rate by which periodic income is divided to calculate present value of income and reversion is equal to the periodic income per dollar of value. In other words, if a present value of 1 dollar is assumed with periodic income, called "d," and the composite capitalization rate, called "R," the equation is:

$$\frac{d}{R} = 1$$

In this case "d" and "R" are equal to each other and, therefore, "R" can be used to represent both the income per dollar of value and the composite rate by which income is divided to determine present value.

Now, consider a situation in which property is bought for 1 dollar, held for a term of years and resold for 1 dollar. In other words, there is no change in value from time of purchase to time of reversion.

Present value of income is: $R\, a_{\overline{n}|}$

Present value of reversion is: $\dfrac{1}{(1 + Y)^n}$

and:

$$R\, a_{\overline{n}|} + \frac{1}{(1 + Y)^n} = 1$$

By transposition:

$$R\, a_{\overline{n}|} = 1 - \frac{1}{(1 + Y)^n}$$

and:

$$R = \frac{1}{a_{\overline{n}|}} - \frac{1}{a_{\overline{n}|} (1 + Y)^n}$$

Remember:

$$a_{\overline{n}|}(1+Y)^n = s_{\overline{n}|} \text{ and } \frac{1}{a_{\overline{n}|}} - \frac{1}{s_{\overline{n}|}} = Y$$

Therefore:

$$R = \frac{1}{a_{\overline{n}|}} - \frac{1}{s_{\overline{n}|}} \text{ which equals "Y"}$$

When there is no change in value, the composite capitalization rate is the investment yield rate.

Assume an income of $8,000 per year for 10 years and yield "Y" $= 8\%$

$$\text{Value} = \frac{8000}{.08} = \$100,000$$

Present Value of income and reversion at 8%:

Income; 10 years $8000 × 6.710081...................... $ 53,681
Reversion deferred 10 years $100,000 × .463193.... 46,319
Present value Income and Reversion...................... $100,000

Of all the basic principles of real property valuation, none is more valid than the principle of change. Market values fluctuate irregularly up and down over the years for many reasons. After several years of ownership, it would be a coincidence indeed for equity reversion to be the same as its original cost. The professional appraiser recognizes this and is profoundly concerned with community, neighborhood and economic trends as indicators of future changes in value.

Remembering that the projection of periodic income is the numerator in the equation for value, and the appropriate composite rate or denominator must reflect the influence of future value changes, the question is; how to provide for them in composite rate development?

Assume it is decided to provide for a certain amount of value decline or increase over a given projection term. Call the total fraction of decline "dep" and total fraction of increase "app."

In case of decline, present value of the reversion will be:

$$\frac{1 - \text{dep}}{(1+Y)^n} \text{ or } \frac{1}{(1+Y)^n} - \frac{\text{dep}}{(1+Y)^n}$$

In case of increase, present value of the reversion will be:

$$\frac{1 + \text{app}}{(1+Y)^n} \text{ or } \frac{1}{(1+Y)^n} + \frac{\text{app}}{(1+Y)^n}$$

55

And derivations for composite rates are:

$$R \, a_{\overline{n}|} + \frac{1}{(1+Y)^n} - \frac{dep}{(1+Y)^n} = 1$$

$$R \, a_{\overline{n}|} = 1 - \frac{1}{(1+Y)^n} + \frac{dep}{(1+Y)^n}$$

$$R = \frac{1}{a_{\overline{n}|}} - \frac{1}{s_{\overline{n}|}} + \frac{dep}{s_{\overline{n}|}}$$

Since:

$$1/a_{\overline{n}|} - 1/s_{\overline{n}|} = Y;$$

$$R = Y + dep \; 1/s_{\overline{n}|}$$

In case of increase:

$$R \, a_{\overline{n}|} + \frac{1}{(1+Y)^n} + \frac{app}{(1+Y)^n} = 1$$

Proceeding with transposition the same as above, the resulting equation is:

$$R = Y - app \; 1/s_{\overline{n}|}$$

Check this with Y at 8% and value change at 20% in a 10-year projection. The 10-year sinking fund factor at 8% (Col. 3) is .069029.

With 20% decline:

$$R = .08 + .20 \times .069029 = .08 + .0138058 = .0938058$$

Income: $9,380.58; Value: $\dfrac{\$9,380.58}{.0938058} = \$100,000$

Present Value Income and Reversion at 8%.

Income: $9,380.58 × 6.710081 ............................ $ 62,945
Reversion, depreciated 20%: $80,000 × .463193 .... 37,055
$\overline{\phantom{xxxxxx}\$100,000}$

With 20% increase:

$$R = .08 - .20 \times .069029 = .08 - .0138058 = .0661942$$

Income: $6,619.42; Value: $\dfrac{\$6,619.42}{.0661942} = \$100,000$

Income: $6,619.42 × 6.710081 ............................ $ 44,417
Reversion, 20% appreciation: $120,000 × .463193 55,583
$\overline{\phantom{xxxxxx}\$100,000}$

The appraiser's function with regard to income real estate is that of analyzing his subject as an investment opportunity and setting a price in which the prospects for yield to the buyer will have market attractiveness. The most explicable and supportable process is to start with a price selected from market experience and test it for yields within a considerable range of future market conditions. When the test reveals that a substantial amount of depreciation can occur without reducing the yield below a reasonably satisfactory limit and that it requires no more than a steady market or modest appreciation to make the yield exceptionally attractive, the appraisal will be persuasive. If the test indicates poor prospects, the price must be adjusted accordingly.

A significant factor in yield calculation is the average, annual rate of profit per dollar of investment. Each of the preceding three examples involves an investment of $100,000 and a yield of 8%. The average annual rate of profit in each case is calculated as follows:

(1) No change in value:

| | |
|---|---:|
| Income 10 years at $8,000 | $ 80,000 |
| Reversion | 100,000 |
| Total collection | $180,000 |
| Cost of Investment | 100,000 |
| Profit | $ 80,000 |
| Average profit per year: $80,000/10 | $ 8,000 |

Average, annual rate of profit:

$$\frac{8,000}{100,000} = .08 \text{ or } 8\%$$

The average annual rate of profit is *equal* to the 8% yield.

(2) 20% decline in value:

| | |
|---|---:|
| Income 10 years at $9,380.58 | $ 93,805.80 |
| Reversion | 80,000.00 |
| Total collection | $173,805.80 |
| Cost of investment | 100,000.00 |
| Profit | $ 73,805.80 |
| Average profit per year: $73,805.80/10 | $ 7,380.58 |

Average, annual rate of profit:

$$\frac{7,380.58}{100,000} = .0738058$$

The average annual rate of profit is *less* than the 8% yield.

(3) 20% increase in value:

| | |
|---|---:|
| Income 10 years at $6,619.42 | $ 66,194.20 |
| Reversion | 120,000.00 |
| Total collection | $186,194.20 |
| Cost of investment | 100,000.00 |
| Profit | $ 86,194.20 |

Average profit per year: $86,194.20/10    $  8,619.42

Average, annual rate of profit:

$$\frac{8,619.42}{100,000} = .0861942$$

The average annual rate of profit is *greater* than the 8% yield.

*Summary of Rules:*

(1) To calculate composite rate "R" when *depreciation* is to be provided for:

$$Y + \text{dep}\ ^{1/s}\overline{n|} = R$$

(2) To calculate composite rate "R" when *appreciation* is to be provided for:

$$Y - \text{app}\ ^{1/s}\overline{n|} = R$$

(3) When reversion is equal to the cost of investment (i.e. no change in value), investment yield is equal to the average, annual rate of profit per dollar of investment.

(4) When reversion is less than the cost of investment (i.e. depreciation occurs), the average rate of profit per dollar of investment is less than the investment yield.

(5) When reversion is greater than the cost of investment (i.e. appreciation occurs) the average rate of profit per dollar of investment is greater than the investment yield.

**Yield Calculations:**

Investment yield calculations will illustrate practical applications of these rules.

The yield on any capital investment is the rate of interest at which the present value of income and reversion is equal to the amount invested.

Since yield can rarely be determined by direct computation because of more than one unknown factor, it is usually done by closely bracketing the answer by use of 2 trial rates and interpolating for actual yield. This can be done most accurately by employing the compound interest functions which introduce the smallest error when subjected to straight line interpolation. If the difference between corresponding functions at 6% and 7% were according to a straight line, the corresponding function at 6½% would be one half the sum of the 6% and 7% functions. Although this is not the case because changes occur according to logarithmic curves, the differentials are much smaller with regard to some functions than others.

This is demonstrated by the following tabulation based on 6%, 7% and 6½% functions at 9 years: Annual Compounding.

| COLUMN: | 1. | 2. | 3. | 4. | 5. | 6. |
|---|---|---|---|---|---|---|
| YIELD: | | | | | | |
| 6% | 1.689479 | 11.491316 | .087022 | .591898 | 6.801692 | .147022 |
| 7% | 1.838459 | 11.977989 | .083486 | .543934 | 6.515232 | .153486 |
| TOTALS: | 3.527938 | 23.469305 | .170508 | 1.135752 | 13.316924 | .300508 |
| ÷ BY 2, | 1.763969 | 11.734653 | .085254 | .567876 | 6.658462 | .150254 |
| 6½% | 1.762570 | 11.731852 | .085238 | .567353 | 6.656104 | .150238 |
| DIFFERENCES: | .001399 | .002801 | .000016 | .000523 | .002358 | .000016 |

Notice that in Columns 3 and 6 there is no differential error by direct interpolation until we reach the 5th decimal place. It is therefore apparent that the error by direct or straight line interpolation will be of little significance where we can use these functions in yield calculations. The third column or sinking fund factor is used in every case where the equity reversion is either greater or less than the equity investment.

Use of the sinking fund factor in yield calculation is demonstrated in this computation for bond yield.

A $1,000 bond bearing interest at 3% payable annually is offered at $800 nine years before maturity.

What is the yield if bought for $800, held to maturity and collected at face amount?

*Solution:*

Interest dividend as % of $800 = 30/800 = .0375 or 3.75%. (Cap. rate is .0375.)

Appreciation 9 yrs. $1,000 — $800 = $200; 200/800 = .25 or 25%.

| | |
|---|---:|
| Interest Collection, 9 yrs. 9 × 30 | $ 270 |
| Principal Collection | 1,000 |
| Total Collection | $1,270 |
| Investment | 800 |
| Profit | $ 470 |

Average profit per year, 470/9 = $52.22+ as a % of investment,

$$\frac{52.22}{800} = 6.5275\%.$$

REF: "When reversion is greater than capital investment, yield will be *less* than average annual rate of profit per dollar of investment." Since reversion in this case is 25% greater than investment, we know the yield will be less than the average profit of 6.5275%. We can therefore start with 6% as a trial rate in the formula which would be used to find "R" = .0375.

$$Y - .25 \times 1/s\overline{n} = .0375$$

| | | | |
|---|---|---|---|
| .06 — .25 × .087022 = .06 — .021756 = .038244; | Target; | .037500 |
| .05 — .25 × .090690 = .05 — .022673 = .027327; | | .027327 |
| .01 | Differences; | .010917 | .010173 |

And, By Interpolation:

$$Y = .05 + \frac{.01 \times .010173}{.010917} = .05 + .009318 = .059318 \text{ or, } 5.9318\%$$

This answer is correct to 6 decimal places; price of the bond would probably be quoted to yield 5.93% or 5.932%.

Sinking fund factors for 6% and 5% are from Col. 3 at 9 years.

The same principle is applicable to equity investment yield.

(A) *Example:*

Jim Higgins purchased an apartment building for $600,000. He borrowed $450,000 at 5½% interest to be fully amortized in 25 years by level monthly installments. His cash equity investment was $150,000. He resold the property 8 years later for $525,000. Net cash flow income produced by the property during the 8 year term of ownership averaged $49,500 per year as if free and clear. Compute the equity yield.

*Solution:*

Annual Mortgage Requirement, "f" = .0738

Sp — 1 at 5½% 8 years monthly table = .551147

$$P = \left(\frac{.0738}{.055} - 1\right) \times .551147 = .188392; \text{ complement; } .811608$$

| Purchase Capital: | | Income | |
|---|---|---|---|
| Mortgage | $450,000 × .0738 | $33,210 | *Equity Cap.* |
| Equity | 150,000 | 16,290 | *Rate* |
| Cash to Seller | $600,000 | $49,500 | .1086 |

| | |
|---|---|
| Property reversion deferred 8 years | $525,000 |
| Less mortgage balance, $450,000 × .811608 | 365,224 |
| Reversion to Equity | $159,776 |

Equity appreciates $9776/150000 = .0651733.

| | |
|---|---|
| Income 8 years at $16,290 | $130,320 |
| Reversionary profit | 9,776 |
| Total profit | $140,096 |
| Average profit per year $140096/8 | $ 17,512 |

Average rate of profit, 17512/150000 = .1167. Equity Cap. rate; 16290/150000 = .1086; (Target.) Since reversion is slightly greater than investment, yield will be slightly less than .1167. Start bracketing at .12%

*Y*

| | | | |
|---|---|---|---|
| .12 — .0651733 × .081302 = .1147013 | | .1086000 |
| .11 — .0651733 × .084321 = .1045046 | | .1045046 |
| .01    *Differences* | .0101967 | .0040954 |

By Interpolation:

$$Y = .11 + \frac{.01 \times 40954}{101967} = .114016+. \text{ Say } 11.4\%$$

(B) *Influence of Financing:*

Assume the $600,000 purchase price was paid as a 100% cash equity investment. Compute yield with income and resale the same as above.

| | |
|---|---|
| Income 8 years at $49,500 | $396,000 |
| Proceeds of resale | 525,000 |
| Total collection | $921,000 |
| Cost of Investment | 600,000 |
| Profit | $321,000 |

Average profit per year, $321,000/8 = $40,125

Average rate of profit $40125/600000 = .066875$

Composite cap. rate, target, $\dfrac{49500}{600,000} = .0825$

Depreciation $\dfrac{75,000}{600000} = .125$

Since reversion is less than investment, average rate of profit is less than yield. Start bracketing at 7½ % for target .0825

$Y$

$.075 + .125 \times .095727 = .0869658 \qquad .0825000$

$.070 + .125 \times .097468 = .0821835 \qquad .0821835$

$\overline{.005}$ *Differences* $\qquad\qquad \overline{47823} \qquad\qquad \overline{3165}$

By interpolation:

$$Y = .070 + \frac{.005 \times 3165}{47823} = .07033 \text{ Say } 7.03\%$$

(C) *Influence of Recapture Term:*

Now assume all conditions the same as in the first example except that the 75% or $450,000 mortgage is to be fully amortized in 15 years instead of 25 years. The annual mortgage requirement per dollar, "f," in this case, would be .09816 and the yield on Higgins' $150,000 equity investment could be calculated as follows:

$$P = \left(\frac{.09816}{.055} - 1\right) \times .551147 = .4325, \text{ Complement } .5675$$

| *Purchase Capital* | | *Income* |
|---|---|---|
| Mortgage ..................$450,000 × .09816 | | $ 44,172 |
| Equity ..................... 150,000 | | 5,328 |
| Cash to Seller..................$600,000 | | $ 49,500 |
| Property reversion deferred 8 years................ | | $525,000 |
| Less mortgage balance; $450,000 × .5675 ......... | | 255,375 |
| Reversion to Equity.................................... | | $269,625 |
| Equity Income; 8 years   8 × 5328................... | | 42,624 |
| Total Equity collection ............................. | | $312,249 |
| Cost of Investment.................................... | | 150,000 |
| Equity Profit ......................................... | | $162,249 |
| Average profit per year, 162,249/8................ | | $ 20,281 |
| Average rate of profit, 20281/150000............... | | .1352 |

Equity appreciates ............269625 — 150000 =   $119,625
$$119,625/150000 = .7975$$

Equity capitalization rate and target; 5328/150000; .03552
With reversion so much greater than investment, average rate of profit is substantially greater than yield. Start bracketing at 11%

Y
.11 — .7975 × .084321 = .0427541      .0355200
.10 — .7975 × .087444 = .0302635      .0302635
.01   *Differences*                124906            52565

By interpolation:

$$Y = .10 + \frac{.01 \times 52565}{124906} = .1042083; \text{ Say } 10.42\%$$

Thus, 3 sets of conditions produce 3 different yields to the buyer. And yet, there was no change in total value, no change in the composite capitalization rate and no change in the amount of decline or depreciation which occurred during the term of ownership. It is obvious, moreover, that these are only 3 of an infinite variety of conditions which would cause changes in the investment yield without modification of the over-all purchase price or capitalization rate.

This generates a question as to just what guide lines appraisers do have for selection of appropriate capitalization rates. The only answer lies in the market. And this starts with knowledge of the money market. The majority of the capital used for the purchase of conventional income property is mortgage money. When the appraiser knows 75% of acceptable appraisal can be borrowed by a typical buyer at a given rate of interest with provision for recapture over a given term of years, he has a factual capitalization rate pertaining to 75% of his appraisal.

The objective of the appraisal is to make a reasonable estimate of cash market value, and the point is that facts pertaining to the availability of mortgage money provide the valid and supportable place of beginning for selection of the capitalization rate.

## Band of Investment Interest Rate Selection:

A plausible method for selection of a composite interest rate is based on the "band of investment theory."

It starts with the prevailing mortgage interest rate and available ratio of mortgage to value. An attractive "prospective" equity yield is combined with this to form the composite interest rate.

Assume, for example, 75% mortgage money is available at 5½% and the appraiser judges that good prospects for double this rate, or 11%, would attract a buyer for the 25% equity position. The composite interest rate would be calculated as follows:

Mortgage Money, 75% at .055................................ .04125
Equity Money,   25% at .110.............................. .02750
Composite Interest Rate............................................ .06875

If a stabilized annual income of $41,250, after provision for recapture, is capitalized at this composite rate, distributions of capital and income would be as set forth below:

Valuation; $41250/.06875 = $600,000

*Distribution:*

Mortgage 75%; $450,000 at  5½%........................ $24,750
Equity    25%;  150,000 at 11%........................ 16,500
        Totals;    $600,000                    $41,250

If the 5½% and 11% rate combination could be established by comparable sales as reflecting the market with 75% and 25% mortgage and equity ratios, it could be used as a standard of comparison for calculating the relative equity rate with any other equity to value ratio and any other mortgage interest rate.

This system would at least provide a means for explaining the source of an equity yield rate. Despite the fact that the actual, ultimate yield is unknown, the appraiser needs an explicable "prospective yield" to start with.

The relationship of mortgage and composite rate in this example is:

.06875/.055 = 1.25

If the differential addition .25 is combined with any equity ratio, "E" and any mortgage interest rate "I," the comparable equity yield "Y" can be calculated by formula:

$$\frac{(.25 + E)}{E} I = Y$$

*Examples* with "I" at 5½ %:

| Mortgage | E | | Y |
|---|---|---|---|
| 0% | 1.00; | $\dfrac{(.25 + 1)\ .055}{1} = 1.25 \times .055,$ | .06875 |
| 40% | .60; | $\dfrac{(.25 + .60)\ .055}{.60} = 1.41\tfrac{2}{3} \times 055,$ | .07792 |
| 66⅔% | .33⅓; | $\dfrac{(.25 + .33\tfrac{1}{3})\ .055}{.33\tfrac{1}{3}} = 1.75 \times .055,$ | .09625 |
| 75% | .25; | $\dfrac{(.25 + .25)\ .055}{.25} = 2 \times .055,$ | .1100 |
| 90% | .10; | $\dfrac{(.25 + .10)\ .055}{.10} = 3.5 \times .055,$ | .1925 |

*Examples* with "I" at 6%:

(Multipliers of "I" do not change)

| Mortgage | E | | Y |
|---|---|---|---|
| 0% | 1.00 | 1.25 × .06 | .075 |
| 40% | .60 | 1.41⅔ × .06 | .085 |
| 66⅔% | .33⅓ | 1.75 × .06 | .1050 |
| 75% | .25 | 2 × .06 | .12 |
| 90% | .10 | 3.5 × .06 | .21 |

Advantages of this method are:

(a)  The composite interest rate by band of investment calculation will always be the same regardless of mortgage and equity ratios:

| | | |
|---|---|---|
| Mortgage 40% at .055 | | .02200 |
| Equity    60% at .07792 | | .04675 |
| Composite Interest Rate | | .06875 |

| | | |
|---|---|---|
| Mortgage 90% at .055 | | .04950 |
| Equity    10% at .1925 | | .01925 |
| Composite Interest Rate | | .06875 |

| | | |
|---|---|---|
| Mortgage 40% at .06 | | .024 |
| Equity    60% at .085 | | .051 |
| Composite Interest Rate | | .075 |

| | | |
|---|---|---|
| Mortgage 90% at .06 | | .054 |
| Equity    10% at .21 | | .021 |
| Composite Interest Rate | | .075 |

(b)  Any mortgage position should always be superior to that of equity because the rate is fixed by contract and burden of management is the responsibility of the equity owner. Therefore, the composite interest rate should always exceed the prevailing mortgage interest rate.

(c)  The risk of equity investment increases as its ratio to value declines. Prospective yield should increase accordingly.

A formula of this type accomplishes conditions (b) and (c) without permitting the mortgage ratio to affect the over-all interest rate. This is as it should be because the fact that a majority of purchase capital can be borrowed does not in any way affect a property's future performance. It only determines how earnings are to be distributed.

## INCOME PROJECTION & VALUATION

Following is the actual cash flow income stream produced by a typical apartment project over a 10 year period. It is noteworthy that year to year fluctuation runs quite high in several places. This is characteristic of individual performance of multiple occupancy properties because non-recurring replacement and maintenance expenditures decrease net income substantially in years of their occurrence and result in corresponding increases in years when nothing more than operating expenses are incurred.

| Year | Year | Year |
|---|---|---|
| 1. $41887 | 4.  40803 | 7.  37914 |
| 2.  38782 | 5.  31706 | 8.  40727 |
| 3.  48036 | 6. $51048 | 9.  37563 |
|  |  | 10.  40908 |

Now let us assume:

(a)  This property was purchased at the beginning of the 10 year period for $513000.

(b)  The purchase capital structure was:

| | |
|---|---|
| Cash equity investment | $171000 |
| Mortgage at 5% interest to be fully amortized in 20 years by level installments of $2257.20 per month | 342000 |
| Total cash to seller | $513000 |

(c)  The property was sold at the end of the 10 year period for $436,000 indicating about 15% depreciation in value during the term of ownership.

The distribution of income would be as follows:

| Year | Mortgage Interest | Mortgage Amortization | Equity Dividend | Total |
|------|------------------|----------------------|-----------------|-------|
| 1 | $ 16867.94 | $ 10218.46 | $ 14800.60 | $ 41887 |
| 2 | 16345.14 | 10741.26 | 11695.60 | 38782 |
| 3 | 15795.60 | 11290.80 | 20949.60 | 48036 |
| 4 | 15217.94 | 11868.46 | 13716.60 | 40803 |
| 5 | 14610.73 | 12475.67 | 4619.60 | 31706 |
| 6 | 13972.45 | 13113.95 | 23961.60 | 51048 |
| 7 | 13301.51 | 13784.89 | 10827.60 | 37914 |
| 8 | 12596.25 | 14490.15 | 13640.60 | 40727 |
| 9 | 11854.90 | 15231.50 | 10476.60 | 37563 |
| 10 | 11075.63 | 16010.77 | 13821.6Q | 40908 |
| Totals | $141638.09 | $129225.91 | $138510.00 | $409374 |
| Averages (pennies dropped) | | | $13851 | $40937 |

This is graphically presented by Plate I showing the types of annuities involved.

PLATE I

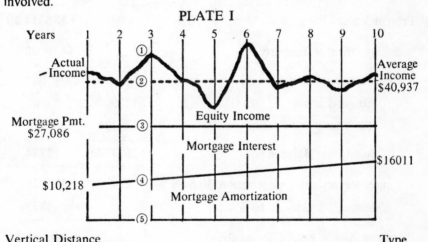

| Vertical Distance Between Lines | Represents | Type Annuity |
|---|---|---|
| 1 and 3 | Actual Equity Income | Fluctuating |
| 2 and 3 | Average Equity Income | Ordinary |
| 3 and 5 | Total Annual Mortgage Installments | Ordinary |
| 3 and 4 | Mortgage Interest | Decreasing |
| 4 and 5 | Mortgage Amortization | Increasing |

The actual yield on the equity investment of $171000 in this case would be slightly more than 10% as will be seen by the following calculations in which we discount each equity dividend at 10% and add the amount of the equity reversion discounted at 10%.

| Year | Equity Dividend | $\frac{1}{1.10^n}$ | Present Value |
|------|-----------------|--------------------|--------------| 
| 1 | 14800.60 | .9091 | 13455.23 |
| 2 | 11695.60 | .8264 | 9665.24 |
| 3 | 20949.60 | .7513 | 15739.43 |
| 4 | 13716.60 | .6830 | 9368.44 |
| 5 | 4619.60 | .6209 | 2868.31 |
| 6 | 23961.60 | .5645 | 13526.32 |
| 7 | 10827.60 | .5132 | 5556.72 |
| 8 | 13640.60 | .4665 | 6363.34 |
| 9 | 10476.60 | .4241 | 4443.13 |
| 10 | 13821.60 | .3855 | 5328.23 |

Present Value all equity dividends at 10% ............. $86314.39

Selling Price of Property ......................................... $436000

Less mortgage balance;

    Original amount ............................. $342000

    10 Year amortization ...................... 129226

    Mortgage Balance ......................... $212774   212774

Equity Reversion; (appreciation 30.54%) ................ $223226

Discount 10 years at 10% ..................................... × .3855

Present Value Equity Reversion ............................. $ 86053.62

Present Value Equity Income .................................. 86314.39

Present Value of Equity at 10% Yield ..................... $172368+

Value of Mortgage ............................................... 342000

Value of Property with equity yield at 10% .............. $514368

Now we can determine the error introduced by treating the average equity dividend as an ordinary annuity. We know that when a market transaction is partially financed by the modern type of mortgage the aggregate payment of interest and amortization will comprise an ordinary annuity. Therefore, the only income in question is the residual income to equity. This is a rather wildly fluctuating annuity. First, let us see what its actual value amounts to as a fraction of computed value of the property.

$$\frac{86314}{514368} = .1678 \text{ or } 16.78\%$$

If we omit equity income entirely from consideration, the error will be 16.78% and any method by which we attribute value to it will reduce that margin of error. If we treat its average as an ordinary annuity, we have:

Present value equity income $13851 × 6.1446 .............. $ 85109
Present value equity reversion ............................ 86054
Mortgage ......................................... 342000
Total Value ........................................ $513163

$$\text{Fraction correct } \frac{513163}{514368} = .9976 \qquad 99.76\%$$

Numerous tests of this type have been conducted against recorded performance of typical, multiple occupancy, investment properties. Clinical material included operating records and market transactions in landlord service apartment and office buildings where year to year variations in the earning stream were substantial. The results proved that no significant error was involved in treating average annual income as an ordinary annuity in a comparatively short term projection.

The term of the income projection should be related to the definition of market value and experience as to the average frequency at which the ownership of property changes hands.

Market value as defined by the courts is: "the highest price estimated in terms of money which a property will bring if exposed for sale in the open market allowing a reasonable time to find a purchaser who buys with knowledge of all the uses to which it is adapted and for which it is capable of being used."

69

Obviously, this contemplates one sale to one well-informed purchaser. Therefore, it covers no more than one term of ownership and the potential benefits which would effect the determination of price would be those one purchaser would anticipate during his term of ownership.

A 10 year projection is recommended for most cases. It is a matter of common knowledge based on general observation that most properties of ordinary investment types change hands several times in the course of a half century. Transfer records indicate 10 years as adequate coverage for the typical term of ownership. There is no way of rationalizing, stabilizing or estimating average income on a total useful life basis. First, because there is no reliable method of predicting total useful life. Secondly, because it probably will encompass future price level plateaus which are far beyond the reach of an appraiser's telescope. Finally, because it is quite certain to exceed the term of ownership of one purchaser as contemplated by all commonly accepted definitions of market value. An estimate of rentals and a budget of expenses with intelligent allowances for vacancies and replacements can be based on contemporary fact and well remembered experience in a 10 year projection.

The appraiser has a much better chance for reliable estimate in a comparatively short projection than in one based on the very nebulous concept of total useful life. The 10 year projection gives him a definite basis for calculating a specific average.

Exceptions to the 10 year norm can always be made when income is fixed for longer terms by leases at equitable rents to financially strong tenants or where the rate of neighborhood transition or other conditions indicate a shorter projection.

The figures in the foregoing example should give us information for development of a formula for finding a composite capitalization rate, including the influence of the mortgage component of the purchase capital structure. Based on purchase price and total average annual income, the composite capitalization rate should be:

$$\frac{40937}{513000} = .0798 \text{ or } 7.98\% \text{ (rounded)}$$

## The Mortgage Coefficient Method:

A variation of the band of investment rate calculation is accomplished by using the difference between equity and mortgage rates as a coefficient of mortgage ratios.

In explanation; Call;

Y = Equity yield rate

I = Mortgage interest rate

M = Mortgage to value ratio

C = Coefficient

r = Composite interest rate

$$Y - I = C$$

and:

$$Y - MC = r$$

This will produce the same composite interest rates but offers an advantage in facilitating adjustment for mortgage amortization and consequent equity value build-up. To illustrate; first *with interest rates only:*

Y = .11;          I = .055;          M = .75

Y — I = C;       .1100 — .055 = .055

Y — MC = r

| | |
|---|---|
| Y | .11000 |
| Less MC; .75 × .055 | .04125 |
| Composite Interest Rate | .06875 |

Y = .1050;          I = .06;          M = .66⅔

Y — I = C       .1050 — .06 = .045

Y — MC = r

| | |
|---|---|
| Y | .105 |
| Less MC; .66⅔ × .045 | .030 |
| Composite Interest Rate | .075 |

71

Equity yield "Y" can be adjusted to reflect any equity value build-up by reason of mortgage amortization and the mortgage interest "I" can be adjusted to cover the cost of amortization or recapture. *When adjusted "I" is subtracted from adjusted "Y," the remainder is a coefficient "C" which can be used with any mortgage ratio "M," to produce a comprehensive, composite rate "r."*

Call the fraction of mortgage to be amortized "P."

$$Y + P\ 1/s_{\overline{n}|} = \text{Adjusted "Y"}$$

The sinking fund factor is at rate "Y" for the income projection term. Adjusted "I" is the annual mortgage requirement per dollar of mortgage including both interest and amortization. This combination is represented by symbol "f."

Thus, the subtraction of adjusted "I" (now called "f") from adjusted "Y" is as follows:

$$C = Y + P1/s_{\overline{n}|} - f$$

The coefficient "C" is employed in the same manner as when interest rates only are involved. And, since it can be calculated for any combination of rates, amortization requirement and income projection term, this formula has been employed to compile tables of pre-computed coefficients and capitalization rates. The scopes of the tables are such that the appraiser can usually find the desired combination and thus eliminate the need for involved calculations.

Nevertheless, it must be repeated that tables are only working tools. They do not supplant judgment. Therefore, a requisite for intelligent use is knowledge of how they are computed. Without such knowledge, the appraiser is unable to explain what he assumes and *believes* when he uses them.

For this reason, detailed calculation of a composite rate by use of functions from standard compound interest tables is presented here:

1. Mortgage money to help finance purchase of a group of retail shops is available up to 75% of appraisal to be amortized in 25 years by monthly installments including interest at 5½% per annum.

2. Net cash flow income is projected 10 years at an average of $32,250 per year.
3. Allow for 15% over-all value decline in 10 years and appraise the property to yield 11% on a 25% equity.

*Solution:*

Reference; 5½% monthly compound interest table; Column 6; monthly installment at 25 years is .006141. In practice this is rounded to $6.15 per month per $1000 to avoid dealing in fractions of a cent. The annual requirement is $12 \times \$6.15 = \$73.80$ per $1000 or .0738 per dollar; i.e. "f" = .0738. In Column 1, at 10 years, $Sp - 1 = .731076$.

In Column 3 of 11% compound interest table, sinking fund factor at 10 years is .0598.

Calculation of fraction amortized in 10 years;

$$P = \left(\frac{.0738}{.055} - 1\right) \times .731076 = .249895$$

Calculation of mortgage coefficient by formula:

$$C = Y + P \, 1/s_{\overline{n}|} - f$$

| | |
|---|---:|
| Equity Yield Y | .1100000 |
| Plus, P $1/s_{\overline{n}|}$, .249895 × .0598 | .0149437 |
| Adjusted "Y" | .1249437 |
| Less "f" (adjusted I) | .0738000 |
| Mortgage Coefficient "C" | .0511437 |
| Rounded to | .0511 |

Calculation of basic capitalization rate by formula.

$$r = Y - M.C.$$

| | |
|---|---:|
| Equity yield "Y" | .110000 |
| Less M.C., .75 × .0511 | .038325 |
| *Basic rate, before depreciation | .071675 |
| Add for depreciation by formula: | |
| $R = r + $ dep $1/s_{\overline{n}|}$; .15 × .0598 | .008970 |
| Composite Capitalization Rate; "R" | .080645 |

Valuation; $32250/.080645 = $399,901
Say, $400,000

This can be checked for mathematical validity by computing present value of indicated equity income and reversion at 11% and comparing the result with the assumed equity investment.

## Arithmetic Check

|  |  | Income Distribution |
|---|---|---|
| *Purchase Capital* |  |  |
| Mortgage, 75%, $300,000 at .0738 |  | $ 22,140 |
| Equity, 25%, 100,000 .1011 |  | $ 10,110 |
| Cash to Seller; $400,000 |  | $ 32,250 |
| Original Price |  | $400,000 |
| Less 15% depreciation |  | 60,000 |
| Property Reversion, deferred 10 years |  | $340,000 |
| Original mortgage | $300,000 |  |
| Less 10 yr. amortization; × .249895 | 74,968 | 225,032 |
| Equity Reversion, deferred 10 years |  | $114,968 |
| Present Value Equity income and reversion at 11%. |  |  |
| Income, $ 10,110 × 5.889230 |  | $ 59,540 |
| Reversion, 114,968 × .352184 |  | 40,490 |
| Total |  | $100,030 |
| Investment |  | 100,000 |
| Rounding surplus |  | $ 30 |

Obviously, the appraiser does not know what value change will occur in 10 years. His physical summation indicates a building value of $240,000. Bulletin "F" indicates depreciation at 2½% per year or 25% in 10 years would be allowable as income tax shelter. 25% of $240,000 is $60,000 or 15% of over-all value. He believes the prospect of an 11% yield after this deduction would be attractive. Moreover, the income to equity at about 10% after mortgage charges compares favorably with other market transactions. He therefore concludes his appraisal presents a price at which the property would find a ready market.

This process is merely a variation of the band of investment method of composite rate selection with adjustment for capital recapture as provided by typical mortgage contracts. Application is made practical by use of tables which eliminate the need for lengthy calculations.*

*75% Mortgage, Capitalization Rate Table at 25 yr. amortization, 5½% interest, 10 year projection, 11% equity yield, shows this basic rate as pre-computed at .0717. The sinking fund factor .0598 for use in the depreciation adjustment is in the right hand column. Thus, by tabular reference, the value calculation would be condensed to:

Basic rate; "r" .......................... .07170
Add depreciation; .15 × .0598 ............. .00897
Composite Cap. Rate. "R"................. .08067

Valuation: 32250/.08067 = $399,777   Say: $400,000

74

## REVIEW OF THE 100% EQUITY TECHNIQUES

Prior to general adoption of the long-term, level installment, amortized mortgage method of financing market transactions, the income approach to value contemplated purchase on the basis of a 100% cash-out of-pocket equity investment.

Assumptions implicit in the several techniques employed under this concept vary as to the nature and duration of the income stream and in the method by which purchase capital will be recaptured. Each variation will have a significant influence on the investment yield whenever a specific overall capitalization rate is applied to a given annual income. In other words, if we capitalize $8500 at an overall rate of 8½%, the valuation will be $100,000 by every technique but the investment yield will change as we move from one technique to another.

And, since the prospect for yield is not only the motivation for purchase but also the only basis by which an appraisal can be intelligently tested for plausibility and market attractiveness, a clear understanding of yield as the critical component of each technique is important.

### Capitalization in Perpetuity:

Assumes a steady income and no change in value. The overall capitalization rate is the investment yield rate. The present value of income and reversion is always the same regardless of the income projection term; to wit:

5 Year Projection; Yield 8½%

| | | |
|---|---|---:|
| Income 5 Years | $ 8,500 × 3.940642+ | $ 33,495.50 |
| Reversion deferred 5 years | $100,000 × .665045 | 66,504.50 |
| Total Present Value | | $100,000.00 |

100 Year Projection; Yield 8½%

| | | |
|---|---|---:|
| Income 100 Years | $ 8,500 × 11.761336+ | $ 99,971.40 |
| Reversion deferred 100 years | $100,000 × .000286 | 28.60 |
| Total Present Value | | $100,000.00 |

### Straight Line Depreciation Process:

Assumes declining income and declining value on a straight line basis. Total projection term is called "useful life" or "economic life." The useful life term in years is normally an arbitrary decision based on nature and condition of the physical property. The assumed annual depreciation rate is the reciprocal of useful life in years. The difference between the overall capitalization rate and the depreciation rate is the investment yield rate.

Or, to put it another way, the overall capitalization rate is the sum of investment yield and depreciation rates.

With useful life projected at 40 years, the depreciation rate is the reciprocal of 40 which is 2½%. The difference between an overall capitalization rate of 8½% and a depreciation rate of 2½% is 6% which is the investment yield rate.

If we start with income at $8500 the first year and present value at $100,000, depreciation at 2½% of $100,000 will amount to $2500 per year. Thus, it is assumed that $2500 will be extracted from income each year to offset the straight line decline in value and provide full recapture of $100,000 in 40 years.

Each $2500 extraction will reduce capital remaining in the investment by that amount. It is, therefore, assumed that income will decline 6% of $2500 or $150 each year.

In summary, our assumptions are; (1) that value of the property is now $100,000; (2) that this value will decline $2500 per year; (3) that income will start at $8500 and decline at the rate of $150 per year.

The 40 year straight line declining annuity is equivalent to one ordinary annuity of $2500 per year for 40 years and 40 ordinary annuities of $150 per year from 1 to 40 years. The present value of this income stream discounted at 6% is $100,000 calculated as follows:

Inwood Ordinary Annuity Coefficient at 6% for 40 years is 15.046297 (Col. 5 annual compound interest table).

The sum of all Inwood Ordinary Coefficients from 1 to 40 years is;

$$\frac{40 - 15.046297}{.06} = \frac{24.953703}{.06} = 415.89505$$

$$\begin{array}{rl} \$2500 \times 15.046297 = & \$ \ 37{,}615.74+ \\ 150 \times 415.89505 = & \underline{62{,}384.26-} \\ \text{Total Present Value....} & \$100{,}000.00 \end{array}$$

The appraiser should also understand any projection of less than 40 years will also have a present value of $100,000 so long as he assumes the 6% investment yield rate, 2½% annual value decline with income starting at $8,500 declining $150 per year.

Assume a 10 year projection for example. Value decline at $2500 per year will amount to $25,000 leaving a reversion of $75,000 deferred 10 years.

The straight line declining annuity will be equivalent to one 10 year ordinary annuity of $7,000, i.e. $8,500—(10 × 150), plus 10 ordinary annuities of $150 per year for from 1 to 10 years.

76

The 6% reversion factor at 10 years is .558395 (Col. 4 annual compound interest table). The ordinary annuity coefficient at 10 years is 7.360087. The sum of these coefficients from 1 to 10 is:

$$\frac{10 - 7.360087}{.06} = \frac{2.639913}{.06} = 43.99855$$

Present Value of Income and Reversion discounted at 6%;

$$
\begin{aligned}
\$\ 7,000 \times\ 7.360087 &= \$\ 51,520.60 \\
150 \times 43.99855 &=\quad 6,599.78 \\
75,000 \times\quad .558395 &=\quad 41,879.62 \\
\hline
\text{Total Present Value} &\dots \$100,000.00
\end{aligned}
$$

### The Inwood Ordinary Annuity Technique:

Assumes a steady income and recapture of purchase capital on the basis of a sinking fund installment accumulating over assumed useful life at the investment yield rate. With overall capitalization rate at 8½% and a 40 year useful life projection, the investment yield would be the interest rate at which .085 would appear at 40 years in column No. 6 of the compound interest table. In other words, it is the yield at which an ordinary annuity of 8½ cents per year for 40 years has a present value of 1 dollar. This can be calculated by interpolation of the 8½% and 8% Column 6 factors as follows:

| Interest rate | Col. 6 40 Yrs. | Target |
|---|---|---|
| .085 | .088382 | .085000 |
| .080 | .083860 | .083860 |
| .005 | 4522 | 1140 |

*By Interpolation;*

$$\text{Yield} = 08 + \frac{.005 \times 1140}{4522} = .08 + .00126+ = .08126+$$

Investment yield would be slightly over 8⅛%. Any projection less than 40 years will have the same present value at this yield rate if the sinking fund accumulation for the smaller projection term is treated as depreciation and subtracted from original value to determine the reversion.

### Hoskold Sinking Fund Technique:

Assumes a steady income and a dual interest rate. A level periodic sinking fund installment is taken from income and deposited in an account on which interest will accumulate at a contract or "safe rate" to provide recapture of purchase capital during the useful life projection. The overall capitalization rate is the sum of the investment yield rate (known as the "speculative" rate) and the sinking fund requirement per dollar of investment.

Assume for example, a savings institution agrees to accumulate interest at 4% on a level annual sinking fund deposit for a term of 40 years. Column 3 of the 4% annual compound interest table at 40 years shows the sinking fund factor at .010523. If the overall capitalization rate is 8½%, the investment yield or "speculative" rate will be .085 less .010523 or .074477 i.e., 7.4477%.

The Hoskold overall capitalization rate for any dual rate and time combination is always the sinking fund factor at the "safe rate" plus the yield or "speculative rate."

# IV

# TABLE C—MORTGAGE COEFFICIENTS

Precomputed by formula: $C = Y + P \, 1/s_{\overline{n}|} - f$

Use; $r = Y - MC$; and $R = r + dep \, 1/s_{\overline{n}|}$; etc.

## Scope:

Mortgage amortization terms; 10 to 30 years by 5 year increments.
Mortgage interest rates, 3¼% to 12% by ¼% increments.

Income Projection Terms, 5 years to full amortization by 5 year increments.
Equity Yields; 4% to 30% by 1% increments.

## Instructions for Finding Desired Coefficient "C":

1. Find the amortization term at top of table.
2. Find pages on which mortgage interest rate appears.
3. Find desired projection bracket.
4. Read across on Equity Yield line to coefficient in interest rate column.

## Supplementary Data:

Right hand column contains the sinking fund factors.

Immediately below the interest rate at the top of each column is the annual mortgage requirement, "f" per dollar of mortgage.

On the next line below, is the monthly mortgage requirement per dollar; "f/12."

The unrecaptured mortgage balance per original dollar at the end of the projection term is at the top of each projection bracket.

**Positive Mortgage Coefficients:**

Although the normal application of the mortgage coefficient is in the equation:

$$r = Y - MC$$

A rare exception occurs when equity yield "Y" is *less* than mortgage interest rate "I." Obviously, this would cause the basic rate "r" to be greater than "Y." In other words, if "Y" were 4% and "I" were 6%, the mortgage rate would cause the basic rate "r" to exceed 4%. In such cases, the effect of the coefficient is positive. Please note that positive coefficients in Table C are underlined and printed in light face italics or followed by minus signs. When they are used, the equation is:

$$r = Y + MC$$

**Problems Involving Use of Table C:**

(1) Ten-year projection of cash flow income is stabilized at $24,342 per year. Mortgage money to help finance purchase is available up to 70 per cent of acceptable appraisal with interest at 5½ per cent to be fully amortized in twenty years.

Allow for a 15 per cent decline in over-all property value in ten years, and appraise this property to yield 10 per cent on the equity investment.

*Solution:*

Table reference, 20 year amortization, $I = 5\frac{1}{2}\%$, 10 year bracket; $C = .0404$; sinking fund factor, same line, equals .0628.

|  |  |
|---|---|
| Y | .10000 |
| Less MC; .70 × .0404 | .02828 |
| Basic Rate | .07172 |
| Add depreciation; .15 × .0628 | .00942 |
| Composite Cap Rate | .08114 |

Appraisal; $\dfrac{d}{R} = \dfrac{24342}{.08114} = \$300,000$

(2) Prospective purchaser of an office building has commitment for a $900,000 loan at 5¼% to be amortized in 25 years. Land value has been established at $250,000. Book depreciation on building will be reserved at 2½% per year. Ten year projection of income has been stabilized at $94,000 per year.

80

Appraise this property to yield 11 per cent on equity after book depreciation on building; i.e., 25 per cent in 10 years.

*Solution:*

$$\text{Stated factors: } M = \frac{900,000}{V}; \; Y = .11$$

$$\text{Depreciation} = \left(1 - \frac{250,000}{V}\right) \times .25; \; R = \frac{\$94,000}{V}$$

Table reference: 25 year amortization, "I" 5¼%, 10 year bracket, "Y"
at 11 per cent; $C = .0533$; $1/S_{\overline{n}|} = .0598$

$$MC = \frac{\$900,000 \times .0533}{V} = \frac{\$47,970}{V}$$

$$\text{"dep"} = \left(1 - \frac{\$250,000}{V}\right).25 \times .0598 = .01495 - \frac{\$3,737}{V}$$

$$Y - MC + \text{dep } 1/S_{\overline{n}|} = R$$

Substitution of quantities:

$$.11 - \frac{47,970}{V} + .01495 - \frac{3,737}{V} = \frac{94,000}{V}$$

By gathering and transposition:

$$.11 + .01495 = \frac{\$94,000 + \$47,970 + \$3,737}{V} \text{ or } .12495 = \frac{\$145,707}{V}$$

$$\text{And } V = \frac{145,707}{.12495} = \$1,166,122$$

Appraised Value, say:          $1,166,000

### (3) *Triple Rate Structure*

Ten Year Income Projection stabilized at $18,720 per year; 60 per
cent, first mortgage available at 5½% per cent, 20 year amortization; 25%, second mortgage available at 7 per cent, 10 year amortization. Allow for 20 per cent depreciation in 10 years and appraise
to yield 15 per cent on equity.

*Solution:*

Coefficients from Table C; 10 years at 15 per cent.
  First Mortgage .0855
  Second Mortgage .0598
  Sinking Fund Factor .0493

|                                        |         | Y        | .15000 |
| -------------------------------------- | ------- | -------- | ------ |
| Less MC, first mtg. .60 × .0855        | .05130  |          |        |
| MC, second mtg. .25 × .0598            | .01495  | .06625   |        |
| Basic Rate                             |         | .08375   |        |
| Plus dep. .20 × .0493                  |         | .00986   |        |
| Composite Rate                         |         | .09361   |        |

Appraisal; $\dfrac{18,720}{.09361} = \$199,979$, Say \$200,000

### (4) *Estimating Prospects for Equity Yield:*

The yield on equity investment will be a product of three conditions:
   (1) Net cash flow income to equity after mortgage installments.
   (2) Time interval from date of purchase to date of reversion.
   (3) Amount of cash reversion to equity.

Although the time interval and the amount of reversion are very important, it is obvious that neither of them can be reliably predicted. The only things we know about them are: (a) the shorter the time interval is, the greater the impact of any value change on yield; and (b) optimum opportunity for reversion will probably occur within the first ten years after purchase.

Therefore, the most plausible and explicable procedure is to derive an over-all or composite capitalization rate, "R" from the best available market date, select a range of yields from high to low and calculate the value changes which must occur at any time during the projection for any yield within the range. When this test reveals that a substantial amount of depreciation can occur without reducing the yield below a reasonably satisfactory limit and that it requires no more than a steady market or a modest amount of appreciation to make the yield exceptionally attractive, it provides convincing evidence that the appraisal presents a price at which the property could be sold.

The amount of any decline or increase in over-all property value during any projection period for realization of any yield "Y" is the quotient of the difference between "R" and "r" when divided by the sinking fund factor at "Y" for the projection period.

When "R" is greater than "r," the quotient will be "depreciation." And when "r" is greater than "R," the quotient will be "appreciation."

*Example:*

To explain this clearly, let us move slowly, step by step, through a simple demonstration.

Suppose a review of recent sales indicates that by comparison our subject of appraisal should sell at about 6.7 times gross rent.

We wish to interpret this in terms of probable yield to equity.

After allowance for vacancies, expenses and cost of appurtenances which may have to be replaced within 10 years, we find that net cash flow income, before mortgage installments, should average about 55 per cent of gross rent.

If we call gross rent "G," we can derive the indicated over-all capitalization rate "R" as follows:

$$R = \frac{d}{V}; \quad .55 \text{ G} = d \text{ and } 6.7 \text{ G} = V$$

Therefore,

$$R = \frac{.55 \text{ G}}{6.7 \text{ G}}$$

The "G's" cancel out, and we have:

$$R = \frac{.55}{6.7} = .082089, \text{ Say } .0821$$

The money market informs us that a typical buyer could obtain mortgage funds up to 70 per cent of acceptable appraisal with full amortization in twenty years by level monthly installments including interest at 5½ per cent per annum. Acceptability of the appraisal will hinge on whether or not prospects for equity yield are sufficient to attract a prudent buyer.

In this case, we will select an equity yield range of 15% to 6%, and our first step is to calculate the value change, which must occur in five years for the 15 per cent yield.

Referring to the "C" Table, twenty year amortization, 4¾ per cent to 6 per cent, moving down the 5½ per cent interest column to the 15 per cent equity yield line in the five year projection bracket, we find the mortgage coefficient "C" is .0909. On the same line, in the right-hand column, we find the applicable sinking fund factor is .1483. So we now know:

$$Y = .15; \quad M = .70; \quad C = .0909; \quad 1/S_{\overline{n}|} = .1483$$

and

"R" to be tested is .0821

Substituting these quantities for symbols, we have:

$$r = .15 - (.70 \times .0909) = .15 - .06363 = .08637$$

Since "r" is greater than "R," appreciation is required and is calculated:

$$\text{app.} = \frac{.08637 - .0821}{.1483} = \frac{.00427}{.1483} = .0288$$

The property value must increase 2.88 per cent in five years for an equity yield of 15 per cent.

Referring to the 6 per cent equity yield line in the same column and same bracket of the same table, we find the mortgage coefficient "C" is .0055, and the applicable sinking fund factor in the right-hand column is .1774.

Again substituting quantities for symbols and proceeding as before,

$$r = .06 - (.70 \times .0055) = .06 - .00385 = .05615$$

Since "r" is now less than "R," depreciation is required and is calculated:

$$\text{dep} = \frac{.0821 - .05615}{.1774} = \frac{.02595}{.1774} = .1463$$

If the property value declines 14.63 per cent in five years, equity yield will be 6 per cent.

Next let us move down to the 10 year projection bracket of the same table. In the 5½ per cent interest rate column on the 15 per cent equity yield line, we find "C" is .0855 and the applicable sinking fund factor in the right-hand column is .0493. Therefore,

$$r = .15 - (.70 \times .0855) = .15 - .05985 = .09015$$

Again "r" is greater than "R," and we calculate required appreciation:

$$\text{app} = \frac{.09015 - .0821}{.0493} = \frac{.00805}{.0493} = .1633$$

Property value would have to increase about 16⅓ per cent in ten years for an equity yield of 15 per cent. It is noteworthy that the required increase in 10 years is almost six times as much as that for five years for the same yield.

On the 6 per cent equity yield line in the 10 year bracket, we find "C" is .0052 and the applicable sinking fund factor is .0759. The calculation of required value change is:

$$r = .06 - (.70 \times .0052) = .06 - .00364 = .05636$$

Again "r" is less than "R," and the required decline in value is:

$$\text{dep} = \frac{.0821 - .05636}{.0759} = \frac{.02574}{.0759} = .3391$$

84

Equity yield will be 6 per cent if the value of the property declines 33.91 per cent in 10 years.

In recapitulation we have:

REQUIRED VALUE CHANGES

| Equity Yield | In 5 Years | In 10 Years |
|---|---|---|
| 6% | 14.63% dep. | 33.91% dep. |
| 15% | 2.88% app. | 16.33% app. |

*The Effect of Book Depreciation:*

Let us assume that a normal book depreciation allowance would be based on a 40 year building life and that 80 per cent of the appraisal would be allocated to the building. The book depreciation rate on the building would be 2½ per cent per year or 25 per cent in 10 years. If there were no offsetting change in land value and if market value of the property should actually decline according to book depreciation, the over-all property value decline in 10 years would be 80 per cent of 25 per cent or 20 per cent.

The result of these calculations can be used in drawing a graph which will cover the market value change, which must occur at any time during the 10 year period for any equity yield from 6 per cent to 15 per cent.

The graphic analysis form is a block of ½ inch squares. A heavy horizontal line near the center represents appraised value or assumed purchase price. The scales are:

horizontal 1″ = 2 years
vertical 1″ = 20%

Therefore, each half inch in a horizontal direction represents one year. Each half inch in a vertical direction above the appraised value line represents 10 per cent appreciation and each half inch below it represents 10 per cent depreciation.

The standard draughtman's curve which most closely fits these scales for the normal range of yields is known as the "No. 60 Mechanical Engineer's Curve"; and of course, the scale for measuring and marking reference points for depreciation and appreciation is graduated at twenty to the inch. A combination of this scale and curve is available in plastic material.

In our example we would refer to the recapitulation of required value changes at five years. Placing the scale on the five year vertical where "Purchase Price" coincides with "Appraised Value," we measure down to 14.63% depreciation and mark the point with a circled dot. We then measure up the same vertical to 2.88% appreciation and mark that point with a circled dot.

85

Next we place our scale on the 10 year vertical, refer to the required 10 year value changes, measure down to 33.91% depreciation and mark that point with a circled dot. Then measure up the same vertical to 16.33% appreciation and mark that point.

Now we have three reference points for drawing each yield line. The first one is at the point of beginning on the Appraised Value level. Place the curve so that its edge coincides with that point and 14.63% depreciation on the five year vertical and 33.91% depreciation on the 10 year vertical. Hold the curve firmly and draw a line along its edge. The position of this line in relation to the depreciation lines on the form will indicate the amount of value decline the property will have to suffer at any time during 10 years for an equity yield of 6%.

## PLATE II

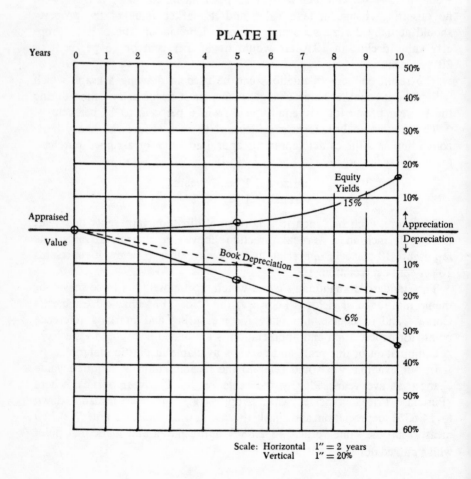

Scale: Horizontal 1″ = 2 years
Vertical 1″ = 20%

Now turn the curve over, place its edge where it touches the appraised value level at the point beginning, the 2.88% appreciation point on the 5 year vertical and 16.33% appreciation point on the 10 year vertical. Draw a line along the edge of the curve. The position of this line in relation to the appreciation lines on the form will indicate the value increase which must occur at any time during 10 years for equity yield of 15 per cent.

An approximation of the value change required for any yield from 6% to 15% can be judged by visual interpolation of distances between the 6% and 15% curves at any point.

Now place the straight edge of the scale from the appraised value level at the point of beginning to the 20 per cent depreciation point on the 10 year vertical. Draw a straight dotted line which will indicate the yield level if the property should be sold at "book value" at any time. At first glance, we can see that equity yield will be substantially better than 6 per cent in this event. (See Plate I.)

Finally, to make the graphic analysis so it can be read quickly and interpolated at a glance, we would calculate required value changes for intermediate yields. Say 9 per cent and 12 per cent and draw these curves on the form.

To expedite the entire process in practical application, we would select three or four yields at the start, enter all the needed factors from the "C" table, and make the calculations in tabular form, as set forth below:

| 5 Years. | | "r" | dif. | | | |
|---|---|---|---|---|---|---|
| "Y" | "C" | Y − .70C | .0821 − "r" | | $1/S_{\overline{n}|}$ | Change % |
| .06 | .0055 | .05615 | .02595 | ÷ | .1774 | 14.63 dep. |
| .09 | .0338 | .06634 | .01576 | ÷ | .1671 | 9.43 dep. |
| .12 | .0623 | .07639 | .00571 | ÷ | .1574 | 3.63 dep. |
| .15 | .0909 | .08637 | .00427+ | ÷ | .1483 | 2.88 app. |

| 10 Years | | "r" | dif. | | | |
|---|---|---|---|---|---|---|
| "Y" | "C" | Y − .70C | .0821 − "r" | | $1/S_{\overline{n}|}$ | Change % |
| .06 | .0052 | .05636 | .02574 | ÷ | .0759 | 33.91 dep. |
| .09 | .0315 | .06795 | .01415 | ÷ | .0658 | 21.50 dep. |
| .12 | .0583 | .07919 | .00291 | ÷ | .0570 | 5.10 dep. |
| .15 | .0855 | .09015 | .00805+ | ÷ | .0493 | 16.33 app. |

The graph is completed by adding the 9% and 12% yield curves. (See Plate III.)

# PLATE III

## ANALYSIS OF 0821 CAPITALIZATION RATE

Prospects for yield on equity investment assuming purchase at appraised
value 70% financed by 20 year level payment loan @ 5½% interest.

| Equity Yield Will be: | If Property Value: in 5 Years | in 10 Years |
|---|---|---|
| 6% | Declines, 14.63% | Declines, 33.91% |
| 9% | "        9.43% | "        21.50% |
| 12% | "        3.63% | "        5.10% |
| 15% | Increases;  2.88% | Increases; 16.33% |

Dotted line locates book depreciation at 2½% per yr. on building.

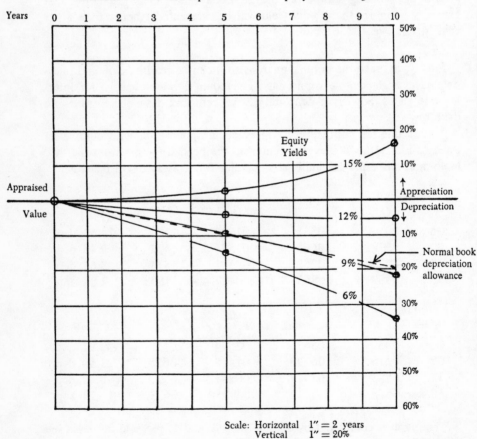

Scale: Horizontal    1" = 2 years
        Vertical        1" = 20%

88

Value changes which must occur at any time during the first 10 years for a considerable range of yields can be judged by noting the positions of the yield curves in relation to depreciation and appreciation levels.

In this example, the space interval from one yield curve to the next represents three percentage points. Thus to judge the value decline which must occur at any time for an equity yield of 10 per cent, we would locate a point at one third the distance from the 9 per cent curve to the 12 per cent curve. For instance, at 9 years, this would be at about the 15 per cent depreciation level.

For any yield from 6% to 15%, we judge required value changes either by the location of a captioned curve or by visual interpolation of spaces between captioned curves.

Required value changes for yields of several percentage points outside the 6% to 15% range can be judged by extrapolation. At five years, for example, the distance from the 15% yield curve to the 10% appreciation level is about the same as the distance from the 12% yield curve to the 15% yield curve. The difference from 12% to 15% is 3%, and 3% added to 15% equals 18%.

Hence we know the equity investor would realize a yield of about 18% if he purchased the property at appraised value and sold it five years later at 10% above that price.

Obviously, we can go on indefinitely reading the graph and speculating as to possibilities under an endless variety of future market conditions.

A primary advantage of the graphic analysis as an exhibit in the appraisal report is that it provides the appraisal reviewer with a quick and specific method for judging the quality of the appraisal as an estimate of market value.

Having satisfied himself as to the property description and income projection, a look at the graph will give him an immediate impression as to whether or not the subject has market appeal at appraised value. If it clearly indicates a very attractive investment opportunity, there is no question in his mind as to the validity of the appraisal. On the other hand, if it reveals poor prospects for an equity yield substantially in excess of the mortgage interest rate, he knows the appraisal is too high. A summary of the valuation and interpretation of the analysis might appear in the report about as follows:

Let us say gross annual rent with full occupancy would be $74,700 and the 10 year budget for expenses and contingencies averages $33,600 per year leaving $41,100 as projected average cash flow:

*Valuation:*

$41,100/.0821 = $500,609; Round to $500,000

*Allocation:*

| | | |
|---|---|---|
| Land | $100,000 | |
| Improvements | 400,000 | 80% |
| Total | $500,000 | |

## Assumed Composition of Purchase Capital & Income Distribution:

| | *Capital* | *Income* |
|---|---|---|
| Mortgage Money, 70% | $350,000 × .08256 | $28,896* |
| Equity Investment, 30% | 150,000 | 12,204 |
| Total Cash to Seller | $500,000 | $41,100 |

## Indicated Average Equity Dividend:

$$12,204/150,000 = 8.14\%$$

\* The annual requirement "f" per dollar of mortgage money is immediately below the interest rate in the "C" table. In this case "f" = .08256.

## Investment Analysis:

"Income imputed to the mortgage component of purchase capital provides for full recapture of 70% of the total valuation in 20 years with interest at 5½%. This reduction in debt should result in a substantial build-up of equity value.

For accounting purposes, a typical buyer would probably take a depreciation deduction of 2½% per year against the allocation to improvement. It is common knowledge, however, that actual market values move both up and down. They never move at a fixed annual rate in either direction over long spans of time. It is not unusual for increasing land values, increasing construction costs and other economic forces to surpass the effect of age to the extent that property of the subject type is resold at a substantial profit several years after purchase. This could easily happen in this case.

Since there is no reliable way to predict either a specific decline or increase in the future value of the property, we have not made any specific allowances for depreciation or appreciation. Instead, we have made an analysis which shows prospects for yield on the equity investment in case of either decline or increase in value.

Among other things, this shows the equity yield would be from about 13% to 14% if the property were purchased at appraised value and resold at the same price any time within 10 years. It would be about 9% with pretty good tax shelter if market value should actually decline according to the normal accounting deduction for depreciation. Since properties of the subject type usually sell for more than book depreciated value, the prospect is excellent for a yield of 10% or better. We believe this would be sufficient to attract a well informed and prudent buyer. It is therefore our opinion that $500,000 represents a sound and obtainable market value for the subject."

## AUXILIARY TABLES Ca, Cp, and Cy

These tables supplement the table of pre-computed mortgage coefficients. They present factors to aid in the calculation of mortgage coefficients outside the scope of Table "C."

### Table "Ca": Annual Constant Financing:

To simplify the determination of periodic installments, some financial institutions quote mortgage requirements on the basis of rounded over-all annual rates covering interest and amortization. An example would be 7½ per cent including interest at 5½ per cent. In this case, the annual cost of a $100,000 loan would be $7,500, and monthly installments would be one-twelfth of $7,500 or $625. Full amortization terms generally are in years and fractions thereof. At 7½ per cent with interest at 5½ per cent it would take about 24 years and 2 months for full recapture.

Table "Ca" presents factors which will be helpful in calculating capitalization rates where the availability of mortgage money is quoted on the basis of a rounded annual constant rate.

### Scope:

Mortgage interest rates, 4 per cent to 12 per cent by ¼ per cent increments.

Annual constants "f" from 1 per cent above mortgage interest rate increasing by ¼ per cent increments to point where full amortization occurs in about ten years.

### Arrangements:

Each tabular page pertains to one mortgage interest rate shown at the top of the page. This is the index to the desired table.

First Column, "f," the annual constant.

Second Column, full amortization term in years and months.

Next four columns, "P," fraction of mortgage amortized in 5, 10, 15, and 20 years.

Last column, constant multiplier of $(Sp - 1)$ to compute "P," fraction amortized in any given number of periods. See Table "Cp" for $(Sp - 1)$.

Sinking Fund Factors for 5, 10, 15, and 20 years with various equity yields are shown at the bottom of each page.

## Table Cp:

This table presents mortgage components for from 1 to 40 years with interest rates from 3 per cent to 12% per cent.

The first column of each pair, captioned $S - 1$, is $(Sp - 1)$ for calculating the fraction of mortgage amortized.

The second column presents the annual requirement "f" per dollar of mortgage based on monthly installment financing.

## Table Cy:

Despite more than two decades of an inflation minded real estate market, the phrase "net income before depreciation" became so firmly established in appraisal education and in the minds of many practitioners that only the heretic would dare an allowance for "appreciation."

Since future depreciation and appreciation are imponderables which cannot be predicted with any degree of certainty, the question is, "Why be so presumptuous as to try?" It seems more plausible to obtain an overall capitalization rate from the best available market information and test it for plus and minus value changes which would produce a broad range of investment yields.

There is no question of the propriety of projecting income for a comparatively short term on a stabilized or average basis by allowing for vacancies and other contingencies. But, what about the month-to-month or year-to-year lease situation where the landlord has a waiting list with no vacancies? Contingent allowances at the point of beginning may unduly penalize the property. We have no way of knowing when vacancies will occur nor do we know that they will not be offset by rental increases between now and when they do occur.

Table Cy has been recalculated to include both the sinking fund factor and an income adjustment factor indicated by symbol "J" in the right-hand column under each equity yield rate.

Combined use of both factors facilitates investment analysis where the value to be tested is the result of capitalizing the actual net cash flow income before debt service as it is at time of appraisal. In other words, there are no contingent allowances or other efforts to project income on a stabilized or average basis.

The analysis will show decreases and increases in net cash flow income as well as corresponding decreases and increases in overall property value that would produce any selected group of equity yields. In other words, yield curves on the graphic analysis form will present changes in *both* income and property value.

Rules for use of adjustment factor "J" are as follows:

For analysis of a given cap. rate "R" to show changes in both income and value for any equity yield:

$$\frac{r - R}{RJ + 1/s_{\overline{n|}}} = \text{dep. or app.}$$

Note: If quotient is negative, it will represent the decline in both income and value for the selected yield. If it is positive, it will represent the increase in both income and value for the selected yield.

To compute overall cap. rate "R" for any given change in income and value, i.e., (depreciation or appreciation) with any equity yield:

$$\frac{r + \text{dep. } 1/s_{\overline{n|}}}{1 - \text{dep. } J} = R$$

$$\frac{r - \text{app. } 1/s_{\overline{n|}}}{1 + \text{app. } J} = R$$

Formula for calculating "J" is:

$$1/s_{\overline{n|}}\left(\frac{N}{1 - V^n} - \frac{1}{Y}\right) = J$$

$N =$ Projection years

$1/s_{\overline{n|}}$ and $V^n$ are at equity yield Y for N years

The reader will probably have little need for this formula because Table Cy covers equity yields from 3% to 30% and for from 1 to 40 years.

In the following example, basic rates "r" and sinking fund factors were obtained from the 25-year amortization, 75% mortage capitalization rate table. "J" factors are from Table Cy. The arithmetic by use of any calculating machine is expedited by entering all these factors on a form at the start.

## Auxiliary Table "Cy"

**Subject:—**

60-unit garden apartment project, 3 years old. Well located in a growing neighborhood. Has had practically 100% occupancy since completion.

**Salient Facts:—**

1. Gross annual rent 100% occupancy    $192,540
2. Audited collection, last 12 months    $191,896
3. Audited expenses, last 12 months    <u>72,464</u>

   Net Income, last 12 months    $119,432

4. Apartments are rented on a year-to-year basis. We do not know what rent and expenses will be next year or any year thereafter.
5. A purchaser can finance 75% of acceptable appraisal by mortgage to be amortized in 25 years by level monthly installments including interest based on 9¼% per annum. The annual constant is .10284 per dollar.
6. Our best advice from brokers is that this property can be sold with the prospect of a 12% cash flow dividend to the equity investor after debt service.

**Problem:—**

Capitalize current income on the basis of #5 and #6 and analyze the result for 5- and 10-year income and value changes for equity yields of 8%, 12%, 16% and 20%.

**Solution:—**

$$\text{Mortgage } .75 \times .10284 = .07713$$
$$\text{Equity } \quad .25 \times .12000 = .03000$$

Overall cap. rate, R    <u>.10713</u>

Capitalized Value: 119432/.10713 = $1,114,832+

               say    $1,114,000

        Adjustment for R, 119,432/1,114,000 = .10721

Distribution:

| Purchase Capital | | | Income |
|---|---|---|---|
| Mortgage | $ 835,500 | × .10284 | $ 85,087.32 |
| Equity Investment | 278,500 | × .12332 | 34,344.68 |
| | $1,114,000 | | $119,432.00 |

94

## Auxiliary Table "Cy"

R $.10721$

| | Projection yrs. 5 | Projection yrs. 10 |
|---|---|---|
| Y | | |
| 8% | r $088766$ $1/s_{\overline{n}}$ $.1705$ <br> R $.107210$ XJ $.5375$ = $.0576$ <br> $-018444$ ÷ $.2281$ <br> = Change $-.0808$ | r $088374$ $1/s_{\overline{n}}$ $.0690$ <br> R $.10721$ XJ $.4230$ = $.0453$ <br> $-.018836$ ÷ $.1143$ <br> = Change $-.1648$ |
| 12% | r $.099406$ $1/s_{\overline{n}}$ $.1574$ <br> R $.10721$ XJ $.5077$ = $.0544$ <br> $-007804$ ÷ $.2118$ <br> = Change $-.0368$ | r $099902$ $1/s_{\overline{n}}$ $.0570$ <br> R $.10721$ XJ $.3655$ = $.0392$ <br> $.007308$ ÷ $.0962$ <br> = Change $-0760$ |
| 16% | r $.109995$ $1/s_{\overline{n}}$ $.1454$ <br> R $.10721$ XJ $.4789$ = $.0513$ <br> $+.002785$ ÷ $.1967$ <br> = Change $+0142$ | r $.111180$ $1/s_{\overline{n}}$ $.0469$ <br> R $.10721$ XJ $.3133$ = $.0336$ <br> $+.00397$ ÷ $.0805$ <br> = Change $+.0493$ |
| 20% | r $.120536$ $1/s_{\overline{n}}$ $.1344$ <br> R $.10721$ XJ $.4514$ = $.0484$ <br> $+.013326$ ÷ $.1828$ <br> = Change $+.0729$ | r $.122243$ $1/s_{\overline{n}}$ $.0385$ <br> R $.10721$ XJ $.2668$ = $.0286$ <br> $+.015033$ ÷ $.0671$ <br> = Change $+.2240$ |
| | r _____ $1/s_{\overline{n}}$ _____ <br> R _____ XJ _____ <br> _____ ÷ _____ <br> = Change _____ | r _____ $1/s_{\overline{n}}$ _____ <br> R _____ XJ _____ <br> _____ ÷ _____ <br> = Change _____ |
| | r _____ $1/s_{\overline{n}}$ _____ <br> R _____ XJ _____ <br> _____ ÷ _____ <br> = Change _____ | r _____ $1/s_{\overline{n}}$ _____ <br> R _____ XJ _____ <br> _____ ÷ _____ <br> = Change _____ |

## PLATE IV

## ANALYSIS OF .10721 CAPITALIZATION RATE

Prospects for yield on equity investment assuming purchase at appraised value 75% financed by 25-year level payment loan at 9¼% interest.

Yield curves below and above the central "appraised value" line indicate declines and increases in net cash flow income before mortgage payments as well as declines and increases in overall property values which would result in the equity yield written on each curve.

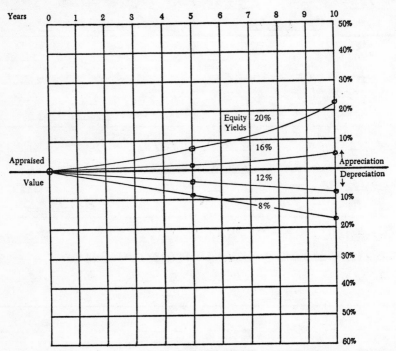

It is apparent that yield to equity will be 15% or better if earnings of the property remain at about the current level.

## OTHER PROBLEMS INVOLVING USE OF AUXILIARY TABLES
### Ca, Cp, and Cy

1. Stabilized income projected 10 years at $17,120 per year. Mortgage money to help finance purchase is available to 75 per cent of acceptable appraisal with monthly installments based on 8 per cent annual constant including interest at 5¾ per cent.

   Allow for 15 per cent property value decline in 10 years, and appraise this property to yield 12 per cent on equity.

*Solution:*

From Table Ca at $I = 5\frac{3}{4}\%$
  Formulas:

$$Y + P\ 1/S_{\overline{n}|} - f = C$$
$$Y - MC + \text{dep}\ 1/S_{\overline{n}|} = R$$
$$d/R = V$$

| | |
|---|---:|
| Equity Yield, "Y"............................................ | .1200 |
| Plus P $1/S_{\overline{n}|}$; .303140 $\times$ .0570.................. | .01728 |
| Adjusted "Y" ................................................ | .13728 |
| Less "f" (adjusted I)................................. | .08000 |
| Mortgage coefficient, "C"........................... | .05728 |
| Equity Yield, "Y"........................................... | .12000 |
| Less MC; .75 $\times$ .05728............................ | .04296 |
| Basic rate, "r"................................................. | .07704 |
| Plus dep $1/S_{\overline{n}|}$; .15 $\times$ .0570..................... | .00855 |
| Over-all capitalization rate "R".............. ..... | .08559 |

Valuation, over-all rate called .0856

$$V = 17120/.0856 = \$200,000$$

2. A supermarket lease providing a net annual income of $21,000 per year will expire in 17 years. Mortgage money is available at 75 per cent of acceptable appraisal on $7\frac{3}{4}$ per cent annual constant basis including interest at $5\frac{1}{2}$ per cent. Allow for 40 per cent property value decline in 17 years, and appraise to yield 10 per cent on equity.

*Solution:*

Tables Ca, Cp, and Cy
  Formulas:

$$(f/I - 1)\ (Sp - 1) = P$$

Other formulas same as last problem. $Sp - 1$ at $5\frac{1}{2}\%$, 1.5418, $1/S_{\overline{n}|}$ 17 years from Table, $Cy = .0247$ $(f/I - 1)$ from Table Ca $= .409091$

$$P = .409091 \times 1.5418 = .630736$$

| | |
|---|---|
| Equity Yield, "Y" | .10000 |
| Plus P $1/S_{\overline{n}|}$; .630736 × .0247 | .01558 |
| Adjústed "Y" | .11558 |
| Less "f" | .07750 |
| Mortgage coefficient "C" | .03808 |
| Equity Yield, "Y" | .10000 |
| Less MC, .75 × .03808 | .02856 |
| Basic rate "r" | .07144 |
| Plus dep $1/S_{\overline{n}|}$, .40 × .0247 | .00988 |
| Over-all Cap. rate, "R" | .08132 |

Valuation:

$$\$21,000/.08132 = \$258,239$$
$$\text{Say} \quad \$258,000$$

3. A single occupant retail store property is offered for sale subject to the unexpired term of an existing lease, and the unamortized balance of an existing mortgage.

The unexpired terms of the lease is 12 years. It produces $38,000 per year in net cash flow. The present balance of the mortgage is $416,972, and the required monthly installment is $2,500 including interest at 4½ per cent per annum.

Price this property to yield 10 per cent on the equity investment after allowance for a decline of 25 per cent in value of the property in 12 years.

*Solution:*

Tables Cp and Cy

Quantities provided by the statement of the problem are:

Income projection terms, 12 years,

$$Y = .10; \quad I = .045; \quad M = \frac{\$416,972}{V}$$

$$f = \frac{2,500 \times 12}{416,972} = \frac{30,000}{416,972} = .071947$$

$$\frac{f}{I} - 1 = \frac{.071947}{.045} - 1 = .5988$$

$$dep = .25; \quad R = \frac{\$38,000}{V}$$

By substitution in the equation:

$$Y - MC + \text{dep } 1/S_{\overline{n|}} = R$$

$$.10 - \frac{416,972 \times C}{V} + .25 \ 1/S_{\overline{n|}} = \frac{38,000}{V}$$

Compute the mortgage coefficient, "C," add for depreciation, and write an equation in which the only unknown quantity is "V."

Factors needed for these computations are:

Sp — 1 at 4½%, 12 years (Table Cp) = .7143
Sinking fund factor at 10 per cent, 12 years (Table Cy) = .0468
P = (f/I — 1) (Sp — 1) = .5988 × .7143 = .4277

Calculation for "C";

| | |
|---|---:|
| Equity yield, "Y" | .1000 |
| Plus P $1/S_{\overline{n|}}$; .4277 × .0468 | .0200 |
| Adjusted "Y" | .1200 |
| Less Mortgage factor "f" | .071947 |
| Mortgage Coefficient, "C" | .048053 |

Thus:

$$MC = \frac{416,972 \times .048053}{V} = \frac{\$20,037}{V}$$

The depreciation requirement is:

$$\text{dep } 1/S_{\overline{n|}} = .25 \times .0468 = .0117$$

Hence, the equation is:

$$.10 - \frac{\$20,037}{V} + .0117 = \frac{\$38,000}{V}$$

And by transposition:

$$.10 + .0117 = \frac{38,000 + 20,037}{V}; \text{ or } .1117 = \frac{\$58,037}{V}$$

and

$$V = \frac{58,037}{.1117} \text{ which equals } \$519,579$$

In practice we would omit some of the explanatory steps, calculate "P" and "C" and proceed as follows:

Income ............................................... $38,000
Adjustment for mortgage, 416,972 × .048053    20,037
Adjusted amount to be capitalized      ...    $58,037

Equity "Y" ..........................................    .1000
Depreciation .25 × .0468      .......      ....   .0117
Adjusted cap. rate ...............................   .1117

$$\text{Valuation:}\quad \frac{58,037}{.1117} = \$519,579, \text{ Say } \$519,600$$

*Arithmetic Check:*

|  | Capital | Income |
|---|---|---|
| Mortgage | $416,972 | $30,000 |
| Equity Investment | 102,628 | 8,000 |
| Totals | $519,600 | $38,000 |

If this arithmetic is correct, the present value of the equity dividend of $8,000 per year for 12 years plus the present value of the assumed equity reversion deferred 12 years at 10 per cent should approximate $102,628. Assumed property reversion, depreciated 25%:

$519,600 × .75 (assumed property reversion)      $389,700

Mortgage balance:

$1 - P = 1 - .4277 = .5723$; $416,972 × .5723....   238,633
Assumed Equity Reversion ......      ....      ..   $151,067

Present value income and reversion discounted 12 years at 10%.

Income, $8,000 × 6.813692 ....          ..  .....    $ 54,509
Reversion, $151,067 × .318631      ...........  ......    48,135
                                              $102,644
      Investment  ......  .  ....................  102,628
         Decimal rounding difference....   ...........      16

This example illustrates the seller's advantage in being able to offer property subject to a favorable existing mortgage. If the mortgage condition were ignored in this case, appraisal by conventional methods in a period of high interest rates would reduce the indicated value of the owner's equity by a very substantial amount.

## ADJUSTMENTS FOR DISCOUNTED MORTGAGE FINANCING

When purchase capital includes a discounted mortgage, the equity buyer must pay interest and amortization installments on more money than he actually receives. In effect, this increases the mortgage interest rate and retards purchase capital recapture through amortization. It also decreases the actual ratio of mortgage money to property value.

If we call the mortgage discount "k," we can calculate the mortgage coefficient of the capitalization rate by use of this formula:

$$C = Y - \frac{f - 1/s_{\overline{n}|}\,(P - k)}{1 - k}$$

Symbols "f" and "P" represent the quantities we would use if there were no discount. The discount "k" is expressed as a decimal fraction, i.e. 15% would be written .15 and 1 — k would be .85.

The ratio of mortgage money to value must be adjusted as follows:

$$M\,(1 - k) = \text{adjusted ``M''}$$

*Example:*

Compute the overall capitalization rate for a 15% equity yield in the following situation.

1st Mortgage 60% of "V" at 5¼% interest to be amortized in 20 years.

2nd Mortgage 30% of "V" before discount at 6% interest to be amortized in 15 years. This mortgage to be sold at 15% discount.

Allow for 20% depreciation in a 10 year projection.

*Solution:*

1st mortgage coefficient from Table C; .0874. Sinking fund factor at Y = 15% same page .0493.

2nd mortgage factors before adjustment, Table C, 15 year amortization.

$$f = .10128$$
$$P = 1 - .436255 = .563745$$
$$1 - k = 1 - .15 = .85$$
$$P - k = .563740 - .15 = .413745$$

2nd mortgage coefficient by formula.

$$C = .15 - \frac{.10128 - (.0493 \times .413745)}{.85}$$

which equals

$$.15 - \frac{.080882}{.85} = .15 - .095155 = .054845$$

adjusted "M" $= .30 \times .85 = .255$

Calculation for overall capitalization rate:

| | | |
|---|---:|---:|
| Y | | .150000 |
| Less M.C. 1st mtg. 60 × .0874 | .052440 | |
| Less M.C. 2nd mtg. .255 × .054845 | .013985 | .066425 |
| Basic cap. rate | | .083575 |
| Plus depreciation .20 × .0493 | | .009860 |
| Overall Capitalization Rate | | .093435 |

Arithmetic Check:
Assume income at $93,435 and value of $1,000,000.

| | Capital | | Income |
|---|---|---|---:|
| 1st Mtg. | $ 600,000 × .08088 | | $ 48,528 |
| 2nd Mtg. | 255,000 | 300,000 × .10128 | 30,384 |
| Equity | 145,000 | | 14,523 |
| | $1,000,000 | | $ 93,435 |

| | | |
|---|---:|---:|
| Assumed Reversion after 20% depreciation | | $800,000 |
| 1st Mtg. balance; $600,000 × .627803 | $376,682 | |
| 2nd Mtg. balance; $300,000 × .436255 | 130,877 | 507,559 |
| Assumed Equity Reversion; 10 years | | $292,441 |

Present Value Equity Income and Reversion at 15%.
Multipliers from columns 5 and 4 compound interest table.

| | |
|---|---:|
| Income $14,523 × 5.018769 | $ 72,887 |
| Reversion $292,441 × .247185 | 72,287 |
| Total | $145,174 |
| Assumed Investment | 145,000 |
| Rounding difference | $ 174 |

# V

# BASIC CAPITALIZATION RATE TABLES WITH 75% and 66⅔% MORTGAGE FINANCING

These tables were computed by use of mortgage coefficients from Table C.

With exception of the few rate combinations requiring use of positive coefficients, basic formula $Y - MC$ was used to produce basic rate "r" as presented by the tables.* In other words:

The 75% Table presents "r" as calculated by formula;

$$r = Y - .75C$$

The 66⅔% Table presents "r" as calculated by formula;

$$r = Y - .66⅔C$$

\* Note: Rate combinations involving positive coefficients were calculated as; $r = Y + .75C$ and $r = Y + .66⅔C$.

### Scope of the 75% Table:

Mortgage amortization terms, 10 years to 30 years by 5 year increments.
Mortage interest rates, 3¼% to 12% by ¼% increments.

Income projection terms, 5 years to full amortization term by 5 year increments.

Equity yields, 5% to 20% by 1% increments.

### Instructions for Finding Desired Rate "r":

1. Find amortization term at top of table.
2. Find pages on which mortgage interest rate appears.
3. Find desired income projection term bracket.
4. Read across on Equity Yield line to basic Capitalization Rate in mortgage interest rate column.

**Supplementary Data:**

Right hand column contains the sinking fund factors.

Immediately below the interest rate at the top of each column is the annual mortgage requirement "f" per dollar of mortgage.

The "coverage minimum rate" on the line below "f" is the lowest capitalization rate which can be used to produce a value in which projected income is sufficient to pay required mortgage installments. The unrecaptured mortgage balance per original dollar at the end of the projection term is at the top of each projection bracket.

### Scope of the 66⅔% Table:

Scope of this table and supplementary data are the same as those of the 75% Table except that equity yields range from 4% to 15% by 1% increments.

### Purchase Capital Structures:

Use of the 75% Table assumes purchase capital would be a combination of 75% mortgage money and a 25% cash equity investment.

Use of the 66⅔% Table assumes purchase capital would be a combination of 66⅔% mortgage money and a 33⅓% cash equity investment.

The basic reason for assuming specific mortgage and equity ratios should be kept in mind.

The margin of security for every real estate mortgage investment is the actual cash market value of the equity above the mortgage. The mortgage loan is never in jeopardy so long as the equity position can be sold for a substantial amount of cash.

Purchase capital and income are therefore, distributed to mortgage and equity with market attractiveness of the equity position as a primary objective.

This does not mean however, that the validity of the appraisal hinges on actual commitment of mortgage money in the amount and at the terms assumed in the appraisal. The fact that appraised value and income are specifically allocated to mortgage and equity provides information by which a prospective mortgage investor can evaluate the effect of any alternative amount and terms he may wish to consider.

A statement in the appraisal report covering this point will eliminate questions concerning it.

104

## Problems Involving Use of The 75% Table:

(1) Net Income of a garden apartment is projected 10 years at an average of $21,800 per year. A typical buyer could borrow 75% of acceptable appraisal at 6% interest to be fully amortized in 20 years.
Allow for a 15% value decline in 10 years and appraise the property to yield 12% on a 25% equity investment.

*Solution:*

| | |
|---|---|
| Basic rate from 75% Table | .07940 |
| Adjust for "dep" $1/s_{\overline{n}|}$, .15 × .0570 | .00855 |
| Overall Cap. Rate, "R" | .08795 |

*Appraisal:*

$21,800/.08795 = $247,868
Say $248,000

(2) Net income from a super-market is projected on the basis of a 15 year lease at $18,400 per year. A 75% mortgage is available at 5¾% to be fully amortized in 20 years. Present market value of land is established at $90,000. Allow for 45% building depreciation in 15 years and appraise this property to yield 11% on equity.

*Solution:*

| | |
|---|---|
| Basic rate from 75% Table (15 year bracket) | .0770 |
| Sinking fund factor, same table | .0291 |
| Income | $ 18,400 |
| Less land requirement, $90,000 × .0770 | 6,930 |
| Income imputed to building | $ 11,470 |

| | |
|---|---|
| Basic rate | .0770 |
| Depreciation, .45 × .0291 | .0131 |
| Overall Bldg. Cap. Rate | .0901 |

Building Residual Valuation:

| | |
|---|---|
| $11,470/.0901, $127,303 Rounded | $127,000 |
| Add Land Value | 90,000 |
| Appraised Value | $217,000 |

(3) Make an analysis of the above appraisal showing overall changes in property value which must occur in 5 years and 10 years for equity yields of 7%, 10%, 13% and 16%.

*Solution:*

Overall Cap. Rate to be tested:

$$R = \frac{18,400}{217,000} = .0848$$

*Distribution:*

|  | Capital | | Income |
|---|---|---|---|
| Mortgage 75%............. | $162,750 × .08436 | | $13,730 |
| Equity 25%............. | 54,250 | .0861 div. | 4,670 |
| Cash to Seller.............. | $217,000 | | $18,400 |

Basic Cap. Rate "r" from 5 year and 10 year brackets.

| | | 5 Year Projection | | | | | 10 Year Projection | |
|---|---|---|---|---|---|---|---|---|
| Equity Yield | r | dif. | $1/s_{\overline{n}}$ | % Change | r | dif. | $1/s_{\overline{n}}$ | % Change |
| 7% | .0606 | .0242 | .1739 | 13.92 dep. | .0612 | .0236 | .0724 | 32.60 dep. |
| 10% | .0693 | .0155 | .1638 | 9.46 dep. | .0713 | .0135 | .0628 | 21.50 dep. |
| 13% | .0778 | .0070 | .1543 | 4.54 dep. | .0811 | .0037 | .0543 | 6.81 dep. |
| 16% | .0864 | .0016+ | .1454 | 1.10 app. | .0906 | .0058+ | .0469 | 12.37 app. |

Book depreciation on the building was allowed at 45% in 15 years or 3% per year. The commensurate amount in 10 years would be 30%. The ratio of building allocation to overall valuation is:

$$127000/217000 = .5853$$

a 30% decline in building value with no offsetting change in land value would cause a decline of 17.56% in overall property value; i.e.

$$.5853 \times .30 = .17559 \quad \text{Say:} \quad 17.56\%$$

*Suggestion to Students:*

Use the above tabulation and book depreciation to draw a graphic analysis.

## The Income Projection; Special Treatments:—

The importance of the income projection cannot be over-emphasized. The chapters on *Gross Income Estimates* and *Analysis of Expense* in the basic text, "The Appraisal of Real Estate" * treat this subject in such comprehensive fashion that the only need for addition pertains to the nature and philosophy of short term projections.

A study of performance records of typical rental properties will reveal income streams which fluctuate irregularly up and down from year to year. Net income will be up in years of high occupancy when nothing more than regular expenses are incurred. It will be down when there are substantial vacancies and when non-recurring expenses are involved in the replacement of worn-out equipment, appurtenances, etc.

Since there is no way to pin-point either the timing or the magnitude of the peaks and valleys of the fluctuating income stream, the best that can be done is to make adequate allowances for them on an average annual basis and thus project the equivalent of a level stream. If this is done on a reasonably reliable basis in a short projection, the arithmetic error due to time and magnitude of fluctuations will not be significant.

The analysis of prospects for equity investment yield normally shows that a substantial drop in market value can occur in conjunction with the lower level of yield rates selected for analysis. Naturally this generates questions concerning the propriety of the level income assumption.

Say the analysis indicates a market value decline of 20% can be suffered in conjunction with an equity yield rate of 8%. Does it not seem logical to expect that the decline in value would be accompanied by a commensurate decline in income?

Herein lies the importance of adequate allowance for income fluctuation. A 7% vacancy allowance, for instance, does not mean that exactly 7% of the rent roll will be lost every year by reason of vacancies. A property may enjoy virtually full occupancy for several years and then encounter a period of competition when vacancies amount to 20% or more. Naturally the net income will be down in such periods and so will the reversionary value of the property. However, this does not invalidate the projection or the analysis so long as the 7% annual allowance for vacancy is sufficient to cover average occupancy for the projection term.

In some special situations, however, the appraiser is confronted with problems in which the projection of an average income level for terms of 5 to 10 years is so highly speculative that he wishes to avoid it. Even though he knows the odds against error can be cushioned by use of exceptionally high yield rates, he would prefer to make an analysis which starts with income as he finds it at time of appraisal and allows for gradual decline or increase over the projection term.

This is a comparatively simple matter when the over-all capitalization rate is abstracted from market data. The differences between overall rate "R" and basic rates "r" are merely treated as straight line depreciation or

* "The Appraisal of Real Estate"; The American Institute of Real Estate Appraisers. Chicago, Illinois, U.S.A.

appreciation rates. In other words, they are not modified by the use of sinking fund factors as divisors. Here are some examples:—

(a) A furnished apartment building, rented on a month to month basis, is currently earning $50,000 per year. Market transactions indicate an overall capitalization rate of 12½%. Mortgage money is available to a typical buyer up to 75% of acceptable appraisal at 6¾% interest with full amortization in 15 years.

The high overall capitalization rate obviously indicates that buyers demand a hedge against declining income and value. The value indicated by this rate is:—

$$\$50,000/.125 = \$400,000$$

The required equity investment would be $100,000.

This is tested for yields of 12%, 16% and 20% with tabulation showing changes in value and income in a 10 year projection. Basic rates "r" are from the 75% Mortgage Table.

R = .125; Mortgage Recapture, 10 years; $165,175
Mortgage Balance, 10 years $134,825

| Equity Yield | "r" | Dep. Rate | 10 Yr. Dep. | Property Reversion | Equity Reversion | 10 Yr. Income Decline |
|---|---|---|---|---|---|---|
| 12% | .0862 | 3.88% | $155,200 | $244,800 | $109,975 | $18,624 |
| 16% | .1003 | 2.47% | 98,800 | 301,200 | 166,375 | 15,808 |
| 20% | .1138 | 1.12% | 44,800 | 355,200 | 220,375 | 8,960 |

1. The depreciation rate is the difference between the overall rate .125 and basic rate "r".
2. 10 year depreciation is the value $400,000 multiplied by 10 times the depreciation rate.
3. Property reversion is $400,000 less 10 year depreciation.
4. Equity reversion is property reversion less the 10 year mortgage balance.
5. The 10 year income decline is 10 year depreciation times the equity yield rate.

In each case the present value of equity' reversion plus the present value of the declining income stream to equity, both discounted 10 years at the equity yield rate will equal the equity investment of $100,000. In this example, annual mortgage requirement "f" is .1062 and $300,000 times .1062 is $31,860. First year income to equity is $50,000 less $31,860 or $18,140. The analysis provides for annual decline equal to one tenth of the 10 year income decline.

If graphic analysis is desired, it can be accomplished by use of basic rates from the 5 and 10 year projection brackets. Differences "R" and "r"

*Note: See also text on use of Table Cy

are multiplied by 5 and 10 respectively to find value changes at 5 and 10 years. The graph is then drawn in the regular manner.

(b) One of the most challenging problems has to do with the appraisal of property which comes on the rental market before there is sufficient demand to fill it. This may occur as the result of a building boom extending beyond current needs to a point where it will probably require several years for demand to catch up with supply.

If the property is basically sound as to location, design and construction, it is simply a matter of time coupled with a good long range program of aggressive promotion aimed at gradually increasing occupancy and earnings until capacity is reached.

Such properties have the same attraction for buyers who can afford to wait as common stocks in "growth industries" have for Wall Street investors.

The question the appraiser must answer is; what price has market attractiveness when an otherwise desirable property is suffering from an exceptionally high percentage of vacancy? He may feel quite certain that good management could achieve a high percentage of occupancy during the next 5 to 10 years but a stabilized income projection based on this notion would be very difficult to support. The experienced appraiser knows that qualified reviewers are skeptical of valuation based on capitalization of income substantially in excess of current performance unless it can be documented by fact.

It is much more persuasive to start with contemporary conditions and make the analysis to determine what progressive program of renting must be accomplished over a period of years to produce attractive yields.

A case in point might be as follows:—

About 8 months after completion a 198 unit apartment house is only about 65% rented. There are 69 vacant apartments. Current operating condition is as set forth below;

| | |
|---|---|
| Gross rent with full occupancy . . . . . . . . . | $487,600 |
| Budget for expenses and taxes . . . . . . . . . | 198,800 |
| Net rent capacity . . . . . . . . . . . . . . . . . . . . | $288,800 |
| Rent value of vacancies; | |
| 69 @ $2446 average . . . . . . . . . . . . . | 168,774 |
| Current net income; | $120,026 |
| Say . . . . . . . . . . . | $120,000 |

109

75% of purchase price can be financed at 6% interest with full recapture in 25 years.

If current income is capitalized at an overall rate of 6%, distribution of purchase capital and current income would be as follows:—

*Purchase Price* 120,000/.06 = $2,000,000

|  | Capital | Income |
|---|---|---|
| Mortgage | $1,500,000 × .0774 | $116,100 |
| Equity Investment | 500,000 | 3,900 |
| Assumed Purchase Price | $2,000,000 | $120,000 |

The following tabulation indicates the average annual rental increase, total occupancy ratio and reversionary property value which must be achieved during the next 5 years for equity yields of 14%, 17% and 20%.

Tested Overall rate; "R" = .06

Basic rates "r" from 75% Table.

| Y | r | App. Rate | Ann. Rent Increase | Assumed Occ. End of 5 Yr. | Promotion Allowance | Required Property Reversion |
|---|---|---|---|---|---|---|
| 14% | .0816 | .0216 | $ 6,048 | 80% | $41,000 | $2,216,000 |
| 17% | .0898 | .0298 | 10,132 | 85% | 45,000 | 2,298,000 |
| 20% | .0979 | .0379 | 15,160 | 95% | 68,620 | 2,379,000 |

1. The annual appreciation rate is the difference betwen "r" arid "R" at .06.
2. Annual rent increase is the appreciation rate times "Y" times "V" at $2,000,000. This is the amount by which net rent (or its averaged equivalent) must be increased each year for 5 years to realize equity yield "Y".
3. It would not be plausible to omit promotional expense as a requirement for obtaining increased occupancy. Assumed occupancy at the end of 5 years is therefore, rounded to several percentage points above the occupancy actually required for 5 times the needed annual rent increase.
4. The promotion allowance is the difference between the required 5 year rent increase and that which must occur to reach assumed occupancy at the end of 5 years. In other words, this amount or its equivalent in concessions could be spent to obtain the assumed occupancy.
5. The required property reversion reflects the addition of 5 times the appreciation rate as applied to assumed purchase price at $2,000,000. If assumed occupancy were achieved in 5 years, there seems little doubt that this reversionary value could be realized.

110

Present value of equity reversion plus that of the increasing equity income stream will equal the assumed investment of $500,000 when discounted at the respective yield rates.

Obviously, an analysis of this type is quite speculative but so are the yield rates. There is considerable cushion in them for errors which could drop the ultimate yield by several percentage points and still make the investment reasonably successful. The prospects should be especially attractive to a buyer in a high income tax bracket.

## Land Speculation

Anticipation of profit from future increases in value has always been a popular incentive for speculation in vacant, non-income producing land.

The value to which the purchase price must increase in any specific length of time for realization of any given yield is a relatively simple calculation when the buyer pays all cash out of pocket (100% equity) and when a reasonably reliable estimate of average annual taxes can be made. The formula is:—

$$\text{Purchase Price } [(1 + Y)^n + s_{\overline{n}|}t] = \text{Appreciated Value}$$

In which:

$n$ = projection term in years
$t$ = average effective tax rate
$s_{\overline{n}|}$ = Future worth of 1 per period at "Y" for n years.
(Col. 2 compound interest table)

Assume a purchase price of $100,000 and average tax of 2½%. What value is needed after 5 years of ownership for a yield of 10%?

"Solution"—

In the 10% compound interest table at 5 years, we find 1.61051 in Col. 1 and 6.1051 in Col. 2

$$1.61051 + (.025 \times 6.1051) = 1.7631375$$

Value in 5 years must be:—

$$\$100,000 \times 1.7631375 = \$176,314$$

However, many sales of land are made on the basis of a down payment with the seller taking back an installment mortgage contract. In this case, the problem becomes a little more sophisticated, especially if the buyer prudently assumes that taxes will probably increase progressively with the increase in value.

111

Solution is simplified by use of basic rate "r" as found by formula r = Y — MC. The required amount of appreciation for yield "Y" on the equity investment may be calculated as follows:—

$$\text{App.} = \frac{r + t}{1/s_{\overline{n|}}\left(1 + \dfrac{t}{Y}\right) - \dfrac{t}{nY}}$$

"Examples"

(a) A tract of land is purchased for $100,000. The seller takes back a $75,000 mortgage to be amortized in 15 years by level periodic installments including interest at 5¾%. Taxes are now 2% of $100,000 or $2,000 and are expected to increase proportionately as the value of the land increases. How much appreciation must occur in 5 years for a yield of 10% on the buyer's equity investment?

*Solution*

Stated factors are:

$$t = .02, Y = .10, n = 5 \text{ years}$$
$$M = .75$$

In the 75% mortgage table, 15 year amortization, 5¾% interest, 10% yield 5 year projection we find;

$$r = .0698 \text{ and } 1/s_{\overline{n|}} = .1638$$

$$\text{App} = \frac{.0698 + .02}{.1638\left(1 + \dfrac{.02}{.10}\right) - \dfrac{.02}{5 \times .10}}$$

which equals:

$$\frac{.0898}{.1638 \times 1.2 - .04} = \frac{.0898}{.15656} = .57358$$

The property would have to be worth $157358 in 5 years. The mortgage balance at that time would be $56707 leaving an equity reversion of $100,651. In addition to his $25000 downpayment the buyer would pay mortgage installments amounting to $7479 per year plus taxes. Taxes are calculated to start at $2000 and increase $229 per year:

*Arithmetic Check;*

Reversion deferred 5 years at 10%, $100,651 × .620921,          $62,496.
Less present value of mortgage payments and taxes at 10%.

| Brought forward; | | $62,496 |
|---|---|---|

| | $10,624 \times 3.790787$ | $=$ | $40,273. | |
|---|---|---|---|---|
| Less | $229 \dfrac{(5-3.790787)}{.10}$ | $=$ | 2,769 | 37,504 |

Present Value of Equity at 10%         $24,992

Penny dropping differential             8

                           $25,000

(b) An 80 acre tract is in the direction of community expansion. The growth rate indicates that this tract will be ripe for residential sub-division development within 5 years. Sub-dividers are currently paying $5000 to $8000 per acre for raw land where new, middle income housing is in demand. It is plausible to expect that the subject tract will command a price of not less than $6,000 per acre within 5 years. The tract would be worth $480,000 at $6,000 per acre. The present owner is willing to sell at present discounted value on the basis of a 25% cash down payment. He will take back a 75% mortgage to be amortized in 10 years by level, periodic installments including interest at 6%. Prepayment privilege without charge after 5 years.

*Problem:*

Assume a resale price of $480,000 in 5 years and an effective real estate tax rate of 2¼%. Compute present value on the basis of a 15% yield to the equity investor.

*Solution:*

Calculate required appreciation, add 1 and use the sum as a divisor of $480,000.

Basic rate "r" from 75% mortgage table is .0901. The sinking fund factor from the same table at 5 years 15% is .1483. Effective tax rate "t" is quoted at .0225. Thus, we have:

$$\text{App.} = \frac{.0901 + .0225}{.1483\left(1 + \dfrac{.0225}{.15}\right) - \dfrac{.0225}{5 \times .15}} = \frac{.1126}{.140545}$$

which equals, .801168, Say .8012

Divisor = 1.8012

Present value: $\dfrac{\$480,000}{1.8012}$     =     $266,489

         Called $266,500

Time is the most critical factor in valuation of land for future potential use. A value growth from $266,500 to $480,000 in 5 years, in this case, produces a yield of 15% on the buyer's downpayment and interim payments. But, if he should have to wait 10 years for the same appreciation in value, the investment would be unwise. He would do better by depositing the same amounts in a bank paying 3% interest on savings accounts.

Failure to make adequate allowances for time and interim carrying charges is a rather common reason for wide divergencies in land valuation.

## TABULATED ANALYSES OF SELECTED CAPITALIZATION RATES

Each of the basic capitalization rate tables is supplemented by one in which each column is headed by a selected overall capitalization rate. Value changes in indicated projection terms for realization of specific equity yields have been calculated, rounded to the nearest percentage and shown under each capitalization rate.

Value declines or depreciation are indicated by minus signs. Value increases or appreciation are indicated by plus signs. In other words; "— 16" means that 16% depreciation in overall property value during the indicated projection term would produce the equity yield shown in the left hand column whereas, "+ 16" means that 16% appreciation in overall property value would be needed for realization of the indicated yield.

Each page of these tables is calculated for one mortgage interest rate shown at the top of the page. The page is divided into 4 amortization term brackets; i.e., 15, 20, 25 and 30 years.

The table for 75% mortgage financing shows depreciation and appreciation with equity yields at 6%, 9%, 12% and 15% and, for 5 and 10 year income projection terms.

The table for 66⅔% mortgage financing shows depreciation and appreciation for equity yields of 5%, 10% and 15%. The income projection terms are 5 years, 10 years and full mortgage amortization term.

Blank spaces occur on the 5% and 10% equity yield lines in the full amortization projection brackets when 100% depreciation is reached. When reliable long-term leases justify income projection equal to or exceeding the full amortization term, equity yield will exceed the rate on the line where blanks occur. The letter "m" appears on the 15% equity yield line in several places. This indicates that 1000% or more appreciation would be needed for realization of the 15% yield.

These analysis tables provide data for quickly judging market attractiveness of values produced by a considerable range of overall capitalization rates. Frequently the capitalization rate derived from market data or one close enough to it will be found in the appropriate table. Tabulated factors can be used for preparation of the graphic analysis in such cases.

### Correlation of Classical Approaches to Value:

The concept of correlation as an arbitrary selection from among several independent approaches to value not only disregards the meaning of the word. It also falsely implies that the cost approach, comparison approach and capitalization approach can each be accomplished without integration of factors common to all. Value is always the product of anticipated future benefits and no method of measuring it can be sound without employing this fact as the central theme regardless of what we may choose to call the approach.

The proper capitalization rate is said to be determined by the market. If this is so, correlation becomes an accomplished fact by selection of the proper capitalization rate because *"the market"* is a very broad term. Among other things, it reflects: (1) the ability and willingness of buyers and tenants to pay the cost of creating and operating improved real estate; (2) prices at which the inventory of standing stock changes hands; (3) rates and terms for borrowed purchase capital; (4) potential yield from competitive investment opportunities. These are diverse but interdependent components of the market. If we weave them all into a single overall approach we will achieve correlation in the result.

An application of this principle is demonstrated in the following example. It involves use of the capitalization rate analysis table with mortgage at 66⅔ % of value.

*Exercise:*

In the process of appraising a 24 family apartment house our investigation has developed the following summary of information and assumptions:

(a) The building is about 8 years old. It has been well managed. It is in a popular neighborhood and in harmony with its surroundings. The area is well built up. New apartment buildings are now under construction in several remaining sites. Subject will be in excellent competitive position so far as any new construction is concerned.

115

(b)  Estimated cost of comparable land by market
comparisons ...................................................      $ 30,000

Current reproduction cost of subject building   $314,600

Allowances for accrued wear and tear:

Structure ................................................    $ 11,400

Mechanical appurtenances .........................    23,600

Equipment .............................................    14,600

Total physical depreciation ......................    $ 49,600

Net building: 314600 — 49600 ...................      $265,000

     Total Physical Summation .....................      $295,000

(c)  Present gross annual rent, 100% occupancy      $ 45,850

(d)  Estimated average, annual net rent, 10 year
projection .....................................................      $ 24,300

(f)  Records reveal 5 sales of competitive properties within the past 12 months. These are in scattered locations and vary in number of units but compete with subject as to tenant accommodations and rent. The ratio of net to gross income will approximate that of the subject in each case. Gross income multipliers found by dividing selling prices by gross rent range from 6.28 to 7.35. The composite for the 5 properties is 6.48. The lowest multiplier pertains to a larger building and the highest pertains to a sale subject to the balance of a high ratio 4% mortgage.

(g)  Mortgage money is available for purchase of subject property up to ⅔ rds of value at 5½% with full amortization by level installments in 20 years.

1.  Select a correlated capitalization rate based on the physical summation and comparative sales.

2.  Analyze the selected rate to show the prospects for yield on the equity investment.

*Solution:*

The rate indicated by the physical summation or cost approach is found by dividing the 1et income by the summation, to wit:

$$24300/295000 = .0824 \text{ (rounded)}$$

Rates indicated by comparative sales are found by dividing the net income ratio by gross multiplier as set forth below:

Net income ratio, 24300/45850 = .53

Ratio
Low multiplier $\dfrac{.53}{6.28} = .0844$

High multiplier $\dfrac{.53}{7.35} = .0721$

Composite multiplier $\dfrac{.53}{6.48} = .0818$

The range of capitalization rates indicated by sales is .0721 to .0844. If we use one lower than .0824, the resulting valuation will be higher than the physical summation and, since a carefully prepared summation based on current costs of duplication is wisely considered the upper limit in a case of this type, we should select our rate accordingly. .0824 is well within the range indicated by sales and it is obvious that valuation based on this rate will be supported by both cost and market data. In other words, it will be correlated so far as these 2 approaches are concerned.

Let us now turn to 66⅔% Mortgage Cap. Rate Analysis Table captioned, "Mortgage Interest Rate 5½%."

The nearest capitalization rate to .0824 on the top line of this table is .0825. Valuation based on this rate is:

$$24300/.0825 = \$294,500 \text{ (rounded)}$$

Moving down the .0825 column into the 20 years amortization section of the table we find the following factors for graphic analysis.

| Yield | 5 Years | 10 Years |
|---|---|---|
| 5% | 17% depreciation | 38% depreciation |
| 10% | 7% " | 15% " |
| 15% | 5% appreciation | 21% appreciation |

with appraisal at $294,500, assumed purchase capital and income distribution would be as follows (rounded):

| | Capital | | Income | |
|---|---|---|---|---|
| Mortgage Money | $196,000 | × .08256 | $16,182 | |
| Equity Investment | 98,500 | average dividend | 8,118 | .0824 + |
| Totals | $294,500 | | $24,300 | |

This is a correlated appraisal supported by the cost approach and market comparison. The gross multiplier is 6.42 which is close to the composite of the 5 comparative sales. The capitalization approach provides for mortgage interest and amortization at the prevailing rate and terms. Graphic analysis of the capitalization rate reveals excellent prospects for an attractive yield on the equity investment.

## PLATE V

### ANALYSIS OF .0825 CAPITALIZATION RATE

Prospects for yield on equity investment assuming purchase at appraised value 66⅔% financed by 20 year level payment loan @ 5½% interest.

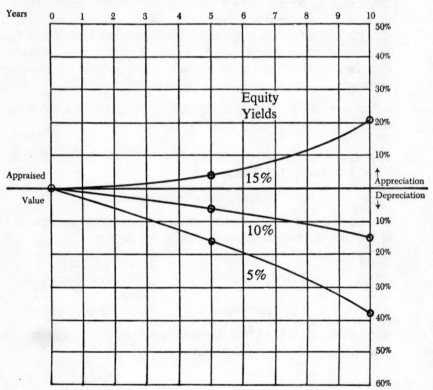

Assuming a typical purchaser would resell at some time within 10 years, our graph shows everything that must occur in the market at any point within 10 years to produce any equity yield from 5% to 15%. Reading the yield curves and interpolating between them we can see many potentials such as:

If the property is resold at the purchase price, the yield will be 12% or more.

If it is sold in 7 years at 10% below purchase price, the yield will be 10%.

If it is sold in 5 years at 5% above purchase price, the yield will be 15%.

If total value (land and building) depreciates 20% in 10 years, the yield will be a little over 9%. If it depreciates 25%, the yield will be about 8%. It can depreciate 38% (which is substantially more than the assumed equity investment) and still produce an equity yield of 5%. Any such decline in the market for this class of property is quite certain to be temporary. Competent management does not sell under such conditions.

# VI
# THE PURCHASE AND LEASEBACK TABLES

Although the real estate market is, in general, an installment market financed by the combination of mortgage and equity money, there is an exception which is growing in popularity. This is the purchase and lease transaction which in most instances is consummated on an all cash basis.

Despite its all cash nature, the philosophy and economics of purchase-leaseback are little different than those of the level periodic installment, full-amortization mortgage investment. Imagine if you will this type of mortgage investment at 100% of purchase price and you have the most important, initial characteristic of the typical purchase-leaseback transaction. The essential differences are that the investor receives a warranty deed rather than a deed in trust; the periodic installments are called rent instead of interest and principal and, he owns the residual property at the end of the lease term. He can then take possession of it, occupy it, dispose of it by sale or lease it as he chooses. This, of course, is a very important advantage if the property is readily marketable and the lease is for a comparatively short term. When the lease with options for extension exceeds 40 years it will make very little difference except in event of excessive inflation.

One other difference which has a minor effect on the arithmetic of valuation is that rent installments are usually paid in advance, i.e., at the beginning of each installment period instead of at its end. In other words, the income stream from a typical purchase-leaseback investment is an annuity due, whereas the level installment mortgage contract provides an income stream in the form of an ordinary annuity. Assuming equal capital investment and rate the annuity due installment and the total annual requirement are a little less than those of the ordinary annuity because each installment is subject to discount for one less period.

The common philosophy then of the purchase-lease investor is: "I will buy the property and lease it to its present owner at a rent which will provide full recovery of my investment, plus a return during the lease term. Of course, I will not have the margin of security represented by equity in a mortgage investment but I will own the property and anything I can get out

121

of it upon expiration of the initial lease term will increase my yield over and above the rate upon which the initial lease is based."

The owner who sells releases capital which has been tied up in the property but retains possession under the lease. In many cases, the initial lease term with its options for extension will reserve the right of possession and use to the original owner for a period of 50 years or longer.

Typical buyers are life insurance companies and pension trusts who are interested primarily in long-term income at a fixed rate of return commensurate with that obtainable from well secured mortgage investments. The prospect for improving this yield through lease extensions and eventual sale of the residual property adds a bit of speculative glamour and provides protection against long-range inflation.

Institutional buyers normally are not in position to or, at least, do not wish to provide real estate management. Consequently, the leases are usually written on an absolutely net basis with the tenant providing all management and paying all the bills.

Although type, quality and condition of the real estate are afforded due consideration, the financial responsibility of the tenant and his prospects for continued success for a long period of future years are of great importance. He will be subjected to the same investigation and be expected to meet the same qualifications as if he were applying for long-term debenture financing.

Having met specifications as to type of property and credit of tenant, valuation of the real estate is usually a comparatively simple matter. Ordinarily, it can be accomplished by dividing the periodic net rent by the rent factor per dollar which will amortize the investment during the initial lease term at the rate of return on which it is based. (Initial term is the duration of the lease exclusive of options for extension.) If inspection of the property indicates that this will produce a value substantially in excess of a well supported physical summation, it is wise to include the physical summation.

Sometimes a prospective seller will seek to raise additional capital through sale and leaseback of his real estate at a rental substantially in excess of that warranted by replacement cost of the real estate. When there is evidence of this in the proposed lease, it is well to note it in the appraisal report. In connection with special purpose property, however, keep replacement cost in mind as distinguished from what the property would bring if offered for sale or lease in the open market. It might include special features which may not contribute to its open market value but may be costly and quite essential to the seller's operation.

Set forth below is a summary of some of the advantages of this type of transaction to sellers and buyers:

To Sellers:

Releases capital tied up in nonliquid, fixed assets for use as working capital or retirement of debt.

Provides capital for expansion or other operations without creating debt.

In cases where a large proportion of value is in the land, there may be a tax advantage as rent is a deductible expense, whereas only building depreciation is deductible when the property is owned free and clear.

To buyers:

Provides long-term, fixed income at a favorable rate of return.

Involves a minimum of management burden.

Lease renewals or extensions increase the yield above the rate upon which the initial lease term rental is based.

Provides a long-range hedge against inflations.

Although the influence of the reversion on yield was not given much thought in the early days of institutional purchase-lease investment, some of the investors are now becoming very much aware of this feature. The earlier reversion occurs the greater its impact on investment yield. For this reason a great deal of attention is now being given to the initial lease term. When a transaction involves property of a readily marketable type, some institutions will quote a much lower initial term yield rate on a 15 year lease than they will on a 25 or 30 year lease.

Two tables are presented as aids in solution of purchase-leaseback problems.

The first table presents periodic rent factors and annual capitalization rates for initial lease terms of 10 years to 50 by 1 year increments. The yield rate at which rent without reversion or renewals will fully amortize the investment during the initial lease term is shown at the top of each set of 4 columns. These rates range from 3% to 12¼% by ¼th of 1% increments. The 4 columns in each set present the monthly and quarterly rent per dollar of purchase price. These assume payment of rent at the beginning of each month or quarter and have been adjusted to reflect it. The annual rental requirement is at the right of each periodic rent factor. It is 12 times the monthly factor and 4 times the quarterly factor. It is captioned CAP. RATE as it can be used as a divisor of annual rent to determine value. And, of course, it can also be used as a multiplier of purchase price to determine the annual rent requirement.

The second table is captioned "PURCHASE-LEASEBACK INVESTMENT YIELD CHARACTERISTICS." It shows investment yields with reversions computed at from 5% to 100% of the original investment by 5% increments.

This table is presented as an aid in negotiating options for repurchase at the end of initial lease terms or for extension of leases beyond initial terms.

Initial lease term in years is shown at the top of each page. Residual values of the property at the end of the initial term as percentages of original investment are listed as reversions in the left hand column. The rate of return at which the initial term rent will fully amortize the investment is in bold type on the zero reversion line in each column. The annual rent as a percentage of original investment is shown at top of each column. This is the monthly rent factor multiplied by 12.

### Problems Involving Use of the Table of Purchase-Leaseback Rent Factors and Capitalization Rates

(1) A large metropolitan area department store organization occupies its main store under a 30 year net lease with 3, 10-year renewal options. Rent during the initial 30 year term is $510,000 net per annum, payable $42,500 monthly in advance. 8 years of the initial term have expired and 22 years remain.

Title to the fee is held by an individual subject to a mortgage in which the present balance is approximately $4,000,000. Amortization requirements on this mortgage have now reached a point where they will exceed the depreciation allowance on the building. The fee owner is in a top income tax bracket. Unless he disposes of this property he will have to pay a tax on the difference between the depreciation allowance and amortization. Every dollar of the excess will cost him about $1.70. The mortgage can be paid in full.

A pension fund offers to buy the property free and clear on a 4¾% basis with full recovery during the balance of the initial term.

What is the amount of this offer?

*Solution:*

Turn to the 4¾% columns in Table IV.

Find the capitalization rate in the monthly section on the 22 year line. It is .073068. Divide the annual rent, $510,000 by this factor.

Offering price = $510,000/.073068 = $6,979,800.

124

## Purchase Leaseback Problems

(2) To finance an expansion program a national retail food chain will buy locations, build supermarkets and offer to sell them on a leaseback basis. Cost is budgeted at $16,000,000.

Two offers are received from insurance companies on a 5½% basis and both with 25 year initial lease terms. One will require rent monthly in advance. The other will accept rent quarterly in advance.

What is the annual rent requirement in each offer? Explain the difference.

*Solution:*

In the 5½% columns of Table IV, we find that when rent is paid monthly in advance with the initial lease term at 25 years, the capitalization rate or annual requirement is .073356, whereas when paid quarterly in advance it is .072848. Thus we have:

| | | |
|---|---|---|
| Annual rent; paid monthly—$16,000,000 × .073356 | $1,173,696 |
| Annual rent, paid quarterly—$16,000,000 × .072848 | 1,165,568 |
| Difference per year............................................... | $ 8,128 |

The difference is caused by the fact that when rent is paid monthly in advance the discount applicable to each installment is computed for 1 month. It is computed for 3 months when rent is paid quarterly in advance. The tenants choice in this situation probably would depend on his preference as to cash position. If it is profitable for him to have money tied up in advance rentals, he will select the quarterly proposition. On the other hand, if he can do better by using the money to take advantage of merchandise discounts, etc., he will elect to pay rent monthly.

(3) In negotiating transactions of this type, brokers are sometimes impressed by quotation of a low rate of return in conjunction with a comparatively short initial term. Assume, for example, a third proposition in the foregoing case from a pension trust quoting the rate of return at 4½% with an initial term of 15 years, rent to be paid monthly in advance.

What would the annual rent be and under what conditions might the tenant consider this the best offer?

*Solution:*

At 4½% monthly, 15 years, Table IV shows the capitalization rate or annual requirement at .091464.

Annual rent payable monthly in advance, $16,000,000 × .091464 = $1,463,424.

125

This is $289,728 more per year than the 5½%, 25 year monthly proposal. However, the 25 year offer involves a total rent obligation of $29,342,400 while the 15 year proposition involves $21,951,360. The difference is over $7,390,000. Despite much higher annual rent during the initial term, the shorter term might be the most desirable because of the much lower aggregate commitment. If attractive extension options can be worked out, the 15 year lease might be accepted in preference to the 25 year proposition.

(4) The central headquarters of a corporation is on land valued at $6,000,000. Depreciation has been taken at $250,000 per year on the building for 29 years as a tax deduction. The cost of the building was $10,000,000. It has been maintained in first class condition and retains its prestige as one of the most desirable office buildings in its area but its book value is now down to $2,750,000. A well supported appraisal for present market value indicates that the property could now be sold for $15,000,000. The owning corporation offers to sell it on a leaseback basis for $15,000,000.

An offer to buy the property for $15,000,000 with a 25 year leaseback based on 5¼% return is received. This offer includes 2 options: one for repurchase at the end of 25 years at $7,500,000; the other grants 3, 10-year lease extension at 60% of the initial term rent.

Assume the following conditions and make a comparative analysis indicating how the corporation would fare by accepting this offer.

(a) Present book value of the property is $8,750,000 of which $6,000,000 is allocated to land.

(b) Seller would have to pay 25% capital gain tax on the differential between $8,750,000 and $15,000,000.

(c) Corporate income tax is 52%. Deduction for depreciation is $250,000 per year. This will continue 11 years when the present building will be written off.

(d) Rent under the leaseback arrangement will be payable monthly in advance.

*Solution:*

| | |
|---|---:|
| Selling Price | $15,000,000 |
| Book Value | 8,750,000 |
| Capital Gain | $ 6,250,000 |
| Capital Gain Tax at 25% | 1,562,500 |
| Net Asset Gain to corporation | $ 4,687,500 |

| | |
|---|---|
| Proceeds of Sale................................................ | $15,000,000 |
| Capital Gain Tax............................................. | 1,562,500 |
| Cash addition to working capital...................... | $13,437,500 |
| Current Assets increase.............. $13,437,500 | |
| Fixed Assets decline.................... 8,750,000 | |

Assuming 5¼% as the minimum rate of return at which the owner is justified in having capital tied up in company occupied real estate, present annual cost of occupancy is:

| | |
|---|---|
| $8,750,000 @ 5¼%.................................... | $459,375 |
| Plus depreciation ...................................... | 250,000 |
| Present cost, owner occupancy........................ | $709,375 |

Of this amount $250,000 is deductible from corporate earnings for 11 more years. At 52% the tax saving is $130,000.

Annual rent requirement, 25 years, 5¼%, payable monthly, Table IV (cap. rate) .071604.

Annual leaseback rent requirement:

| | |
|---|---|
| $15,000,000 × .071604 ............................ | $1,074,060 |
| Present depreciation deduction...................... | 250,000 |
| Gain in deduction for taxes.......................... | $ 824,060 |
| Gain in tax saving at 52%............................ | 428,511 |
| Net comparative cost of occupancy— $1,074,060 − $428,511 ......................... | $ 645,549 |

This all boils down to the condition that if this transaction is consummated the corporation will be paying out $645,549 more cash per year than it does in its present situation. As an offset to this, it will increase its cash working capital $13,437,500. Decision should rest on whether or not it is reasonable to expect that this change in the capital structure of the corporation will increase its overall operating profit by more than $645,549 per year.

### Problems Involving Use of Purchase-Leaseback Investment Yield Table

(1) A warehouse is purchased subject to a net lease which will fully amortize the investment in 15 years at 3¾%. The seller wants an option to repurchase at the end of 15 years and the buyer is willing to grant such an option at a price to yield 7% on the investment.
 What price is quoted for repurchase?

*Solution:*

Turn to "Lease Term 15 years" table.

In column where 3.75 appears on the zero reversion line, read down to the reversion bracket in which 7% would occur. In this case 6.84% appears on the 50% reversion line and 7.06% is on the 55% reversion line. A 5% difference in reversion produces 22 basis points difference in yield. Mental interpolation indicates that sale of the property at the end of 15 years for 54% of the original investment will result in a yield of slightly more than 7%. Quote 54% of original investment as the repurchase price.

(2) A property is purchased subject to a 25 year net lease which will fully amortize the investment at 5%. The lessee wants an option for an additional 25 years at a reduced rental. The lessor is willing to grant such option on the basis of a 6¼% investment yield with no allowance for residual value at the end of 50 years.

Compute the extension rent as a percentage of original investment.

*Solution:*

Turn to "Lease Term 25 Years" table.

In 5.00% zero reversion column 6.27% yield appears at 55% reversion. The annual rent factor required for full amortization in 25 years at 6.25% is 7.875%. Multiply this factor by 55%.

$$.55 \times .07875 = .0433$$

If rent is paid at the rate of 4.33% per year computed against the original investment during the 25 year extension period, the yield will slightly exceed 6¼% before allowance for 50 year residual.

Example:

Original Investment ............................ $1,000,000
Rent per month 1st 25 years @ 5.00%

$$\frac{1000000 \times .06986}{12}$$ .................... $ 5,821.67

Rent per month next 25 years

$$\frac{1000000 \times .0433}{12}$$ .................... $ 3,608.33

The value of this 50 year income stream at 6¼% is $1,002,830.60.

(3) A property is purchased subject to a 20 year net lease which will completely amortize the investment at 4¾%. The lessee wants an option for 3 ten year extensions with reductions at the beginning of

each extension period. The lessor is willing to grant this on the basis of a 6½% yield before allowance for the 50 year residual.

Quote the monthly rent on a $2,000,000 investment for the initial lease term and each of the 10 year extensions with the 2nd extension 10% less than the 1st extension and the 3rd extension 20% less than the 1st extension.

*Solution:*

Refer to "Lease Term 20 Years" table.
Rent during initial term
$$\frac{2000000 \times .07725}{12}$$ .............. per mo.   $12,875

Table shows 6.40% yield with 45% reversion and 6.55% yield with 50% reversion. The differential is 3 basis points in yield for each 1% increase in reversion. Thus, a reversion of .483 would produce a yield of approximately 6½% and the value of the extension rents should equal 48.3% of the original investment at 6½%.

Reversion   $2,000,000 × .483 = $966,000

Call 1st extension rent, d; 2nd extension rent, .90d; 3rd extension rent, .80d and solve for d at 6½% converted monthly as an annuity due. In effect, we have .80d for 360 months, plus .10d for 120 months and 240 months.

Therefore,

.80d × 159.0678 + .10d (88.5455 + 134.8515) = $966.000
149.59394d = $966,000

$$d = \frac{966000}{149.59394} = 6457.48$$

| | | |
|---|---|---|
| Monthly Rent 1st extension | ................................. | $6,457.48 |
| Monthly Rent 2nd extension—6457.48 × .90 | ..... | 5,811.73 |
| Monthly Rent 3rd extension—6457.48 × .80 | ..... | 5,165.98 |

## Long Range Residuals

After customary allowances for depreciation, residual values removed 40 or more years from date of investment add little to the yield. And, since the actual amount recoverable through liquidation in the distant future can be nothing more than a rough guess, it seems more prudent to consider it as a feature which adds speculative glamour to the investment rather than one whose effect on yield can be measured mathematically at the point of beginning.

In problems 2 and 3 residuals deferred 50 years at 100% of the original investment would increase the yield about 30 basis points and, of course, any fraction of 100% would reduce this differential proportionately.

## Problems Involving Use of
## Standard Compound Interest Tables

(1) There is a type of problem in this field which is becoming increasingly common and where the services of competent appraisers are in demand. This has to do with cases where the initial lease terms are of such short duration that analyses of the reversionary potentials are required for determination of acceptable prices.

The following situation represents this type of assignment. Eight years ago a district office building was erected and leased to Standard Oil Co. The initial lease term was 25 years with 2 renewal options for 10 years each. Net rent is $173,450 per annum, payable $43,362.50 quarterly in advance. Income tax shelter by use of the double declining balance method has been reduced to a point where the owner finds his take home net unsatisfactory. He wants to sell.

Although the unexpired balance of the initial lease term is only 17 years, the trustee of a pension fund is willing to buy on the basis of reasonably certain prospects for a yield of 5¾% or better. Full recapture at 5¾% in 17 years from lease income alone would require purchase at about $1,900,000 which is substantially below an acceptable price for the property.

An appraiser is assigned the job of investment analysis and price recommendation. His investigation produces the following initial information and reasoning.

The site comprises about 2½ acres on a broad avenue convenient to the central business district. The street was formerly one of fine mansions on large plots. For several years it has been in transition to professional offices, insurance company branches and district headquarters of large corporations. Most recent sales of comparable sites and asking prices for the few remaining parcels indicate a current land value of $400,000 for the subject site. There are good reasons to expect that this will increase during the next 17 years; at least, it seems perfectly safe to assume that it will not decline.

The improvement is a very attractive, modern, reinforced concrete, centrally air conditioned office building. It cost about $2,000,000 to build and could not be reproduced today for less than $2,325,000.

The tenant has been an excellent housekeeper. Physically, it provides a convenient, comfortable and pleasant place in which to work.

It will last as long as the present quality of maintenance is employed. In all probability its useful life will be terminated by economic conditions rather than physical durability. In this case, it is likely that the land value will have increased to a point where more intensive development is warranted.

If the tenant does not exercise the renewal option at the end of 17 years, the owner will come into possession of a vacant building. Of all reversionary prospects, this is probably the least desirable. It is not likely to happen if prices and rents continue to increase In this event, the tenant would probably take advantage of the renewal option and profit by subletting if he no longer needs the space for his own use. Renewal options give rights of possession to the present tenant for the next 37 years. Thus, a present buyer should expect to have to wait at least that long before he could realize any benefit from inflation.

If the property is vacated in 17 years, it may take some time to find another tenant. However, the building is one which could be subdivided for multiple occupancy without prohibitive cost. Thus, there is every reason to believe that it will have substantial value even if vacated upon expiration of the initial lease term. On the basis of this reasoning, the appraiser decides that a 50% decline from present value of the improvement represents a maximum plausible allowance for depreciation. This should cover any physical deterioration which may occur during the next 17 years and provide for remodelling and re-renting.

The appraiser prices the property to yield 5¾% on the basis of a 17 year projection with 50% decline in improvement value. This price is then subjected to analysis for higher yields within the range of reasonable assumptions as to other income terms and reversionary possibilities.

The annual rent is adjusted to reflect the quarterly payment in advance feature by using the quarterly payment base at 5¾% as a multiplier.

$$\$173,450 \times 1.014375 = \$175,943$$

The quarterly sinking fund factor at 5¾% (Col. 3 at 17 years), is multiplied by 4 for use in the provision for depreciation on an annual basis.

$$.008769 \times 4 = .035076$$

| | |
|---|---:|
| Adjusted income | $ 175,943 |
| Less land requirement $400,000 × .0575 | 23,000 |
| Income imputed to building | $ 152,943 |

| | |
|---|---|
| Minimum Yield Rate.......................................... | .057500 |
| Plus adjustment for 50% depreciation; | |
| .50 × .035076 ............................................. | .017538 |
| Cap. Rate applicable to building.......................... | .075038 |
| Building Residual Valuation: $152,943/.075038.... | $2,038,207 |
| Add Land Value ............................................. | 400,000 |
| Total ..................................................... | $2,438,207 |
| Rounded to ............................................... | $2,438,000 |

The appraiser starts his analysis by assuming purchase at $2,438,000 allocated as follows:

| | | |
|---|---|---|
| Land ................................................. | $ 400,000 | .1641 |
| Improvement ....................................... | 2,038,000 | .8359 |
| Total ............................................ | $2,438,000 | 1.0000 |

Assumed 17 year Reversion:

| | |
|---|---|
| Land ............................................... | $ 400,000 |
| Improvement 50% depreciated.............. | 1,019,000 |
| Total ............................................ | $1,419,000 |

Present Value of 17 year income and assumed reversion at 5¾% converted quarterly (factors from Cols. 5 and 4; 5¾% quarterly compound interest table):

| | |
|---|---|
| Income: $43,362.50 × 1.014375 × 43.208482 ............ | $1,900,561 |
| Assumed Reversion: $1,419,000 × .378878 .................. | 537,628 |
| Total ................................................. | $2,438,189 |

Reversionary requirements for other investment yields under various possibilities:

I. Assuming termination of Lease at end of 17 years

| Yield | A<br>Present<br>Val. of<br>Income | B<br>Required<br>Present<br>Value of<br>Reversion | C<br>Required<br>Reversion | D<br>Equivalent<br>Building<br>Depreciation | |
|---|---|---|---|---|---|
| 6% | $1,868,095 | $569,905 | $1,568,532 | $869,468 | 42.66% |
| 6¼% | 1,836,458 | 601,542 | 1,726,379 | 711,621 | 34.92% |
| 6½% | 1,805,625 | 632,375 | 1,892,399 | 545,601 | 26.77% |
| 7% | 1,746,276 | 691,724 | 2,250,470 | 187,530 | 9.20% |

II. Assuming one 10 year Renewal Option Exercised. Income Stream continues 27 years. Reversion deferred 27 years.

| | | | | |
|---|---|---|---|---|
| 6½% | $2,236,269 | $201,731 | $1,150,358 | $1,287,642 | 63.18% |
| 6¾% | 2,184,206 | 253,794 | 1,546,603 | 891,397 | 43.74% |
| 7% | 2,134,057 | 303,943 | 1,979,289 | 458,711 | 22.51% |

III. Assuming both 10 year Renewal Options Exercised. Income Stream continues 37 years. Reversion deferred 37 years.

| | | | | |
|---|---|---|---|---|
| 6¾% | $2,393,440 | $ 44,560 | $ 530,329 | $1,907,671 | 93.61% |
| 7% | 2,327,793 | 110,207 | 1,436,491 | 1,101,509 | 49.14% |
| | | | | Appreciation | |
| 7½% | 2,205,309 | 232,691 | 3,637,371 | 1,199,371 | 49.20% |

Column "B" in these tabulations is the difference between the assumed purchase price $2,438,000 and the present value of income as shown in Column "A." Since this difference must represent the present value of reversion at the end of each income projection, it must be multiplied by the value to which 1 dollar will grow at the stated yield rate over the projection term (Col. 1 quarterly tables). The product of this multiplication shown in Column "C" is the residual value the property must have at the end of the income projection to produce the corresponding yield. The difference between this required reversion and $2,438,000 shown in Column "D" is the amount of value decline or depreciation the property must suffer. It is also expressed as a percentage of $2,038,000 allocated to the improvement.

The analysis indicates a probable yield range of 6% to 7% with almost certainty that it will not fall below 5¾%. The property can suffer some loss in value over each income projection and still produce a yield of 7%. Its value would have to increase about 49% over the next 37 years for a yield of 7½%. Of course, this is not impossible either, in the light of what has happened to property values during the past 37 years.

## To Calculate Required Reversion:

(2) The amount of reversionary value required for any selected investment yield can be calculated by use of the following formula:

$$V [(1 + i)^n - d(1 + i)^s\overline{n}] = \text{Required Reversion}$$

In which:

$V$ = Purchase Price

$(1 + i)$ = The base; i.e., 1 plus effective yield rate or "Y" divided by number of rent installments per year.

$n$ = Number of rent installments in lease term.

$d$ = Periodic rent per dollar of purchase price.

$s_{\overline{n}|}$ = Future worth of 1 dollar per period at rate "i" for "n" periods (Col. 2, compound interest table).

*Exercise:*

A lease which will expire in 16 years provides rent at $6,573 payable monthly in advance. A prospective buyer is considering purchase at $1,000,000. What reversion at the end of 16 years will give him a yield of 6½%?

*Solution:*

$$d = 6573/1,000,000 = .006573$$

From 6½% *monthly* compound interest table:

(Col. 1) Base = 1.005417 at 16 years $(1 + i)^{192} = 2.821288$

(Col. 2) $s_{\overline{n}|}$ at 16 years = 336.237757

Multiplier of V equals:

$$2.821288 - (.006573 \times 1.005417 \times 336.237757)$$

which equals;

$$2.821288 - 2.222027 = .599261$$

Required Reversion:

$$\$1,000,000 \times .599261 = \$599261$$

# Notes

# Notes

# Notes

# Notes

# Notes

# Notes

# Notes

# Notes

# Notes

# Notes

# Notes

# Notes